THE LIFE THAT LISTENS

THE LIFE THAT LISTENS

BILL J. VAMOS

A Workbook for Personal Meditation
and Group Dialogue

WORD BOOKS
PUBLISHER
WACO, TEXAS

To my father,
Frank S. Vamos
Dec. 11, 1903–June 22, 1979

Acknowledgments

There are two processes at work in the writing of a book—first it is conceived and nurtured, then it is born—the heartbeat of an idea flows into words.

I want to especially thank Reuel Howe, my mentor and friend, for planting the seeds of this book and encouraging me in its writing. I am also grateful to John Killinger of Vanderbilt Divinity School whose teaching motivated me to listen to people before I preach to them. I thank the people of The First Presbyterian Church of Elkhart, Indiana, and the members of the "Feed-Forward" Groups, for being generous and loving companions in the life together that spawned my writing. And to the members of Wellspring Mission Group of The Church of the Saviour in Washington, D.C., who introduced me to the power of silence, and especially to Carol Fitch, my spiritual director, I owe an enormous debt of gratitude.

The task of putting words on paper, with precision and continuity, and finally delivering them in print, cannot be accomplished without the help of many people. I cannot give enough praise to Jo Vamos, for her adventuresome spirit which supported me, her honest and helpful criticism which informed me, and her loving devotion to being my wife.

A huge thank-you goes to Becky, Jeffrey and Susan Vamos, for enduring my times of writing out loud, and for providing me with laughter when I became too serious. I owe a special thanks to Bob Bolles, grammarian and friend, who reviewed and evaluated the manuscript in its formative stages and made several excellent suggestions. His astute and sensitive assistance is a gift I treasure very deeply. I also want to thank G. Harold Silvius, for spending several hours going over my manuscript and giving me his perspective as an experienced writer. I am abundantly grateful to Gwen Alexander for her typing and retyping of the manuscript and for her consistent encouragement. I also express my gratitude to Jean Culpepper for her thoughtfulness and efficiency in accepting and fulfilling the task of being my secretary on Sanibel Island. And, as this book reaches you, the reader, I want to thank Word Books, Publisher, and especially my editor, Al Bryant, and the other people there who helped in this exciting and I hope beneficial adventure.

CONTENTS

Introduction
(Some Ways to Use This Book)

This book grew out of two life experiences.

The first was a preacher's experiment. I decided to ask small groups of persons, belonging to the church I serve, to explore with me the following "words in contrast":

Alone and Belonging
  Work and Play
    Noise and Silence

Woman and Man
  Permanence and Change
    Weakness and Strength

Black and White
  Doubt and Faith
  Want and Need

I worked with a different group of persons on each triad, at intervals of two months. Each of these "Feed-Forward" groups worked with me in a preliminary get-acquainted session and three subsequent gatherings. In each case my co-workers had a hand in selecting themes.

The members of the groups reveled in the opportunity to feed me thoughts and anecdotes from their own lives, investing their time and effort in sharing the building of the foundations of a sermon.

I found the process venturesome. Their life stories, their

experiences, biblical theology, and my own research and reflection became the strands which were woven into the sermon that finally issued from the pulpit, and, I hope, reached the pew.

While working with the "Feed-Forward" groups, a second thing happened to me. I found that I could open myself to God by daily setting aside one hour for silence and meditation. For much of my adult life, I've thought seriously about a devotional life. I thought about it, but never before have I kept it with any consistency. During the last three years, I've used a process advocated by The Church of the Saviour, in Washington, D.C., and "grown" in me by the Wellspring Mission Group of that church.[1] I've discovered that I can commune with God, who is the living, daily Companion, and that his mission for my life grows out of this personal communion.

The two experiences supported each other (they continue to do so). I found myself moving between "Word" and "world" (although the painful, rocky places were and are there, as ever). Building sermons that developed out of my people's real struggles with this world; and meditating quietly, daily, upon the Holy Center of God's life within us, became a hauntingly dynamic and unifying experience. The journey was so invigorating that it seemed worth sharing.

I decided to risk the exciting, arduous adventure of creating the written word. After performing diagnosis and even surgery on the Feed-Forward sermons, I continued the process with new research. I pondered how to express myself, not as the writer of my book, but as the reader. Then I began to write, not for the pulpit, but for the printed page.

So you may ask: what's in all that for me? My answer is: many things. Explore with me some of the reasons for reading this book. See if one of them attracts you.

Reading Refreshment: If you are looking for some fun, a challenge to your thinking, and a new walk with God in Jesus Christ, I believe you will find that these pages stimulate and support your quest.

Personal Meditation: This book is designed to develop and deepen your personal communion with God. It may be that you already have a disciplined devotional life or would like to begin one. Chapter 2 contains concise and specific guidelines on how to grow your own daily devotions. I have included a workable plan for continuing your devotions beyond a few days or weeks. The "Steps into Silence" in chapter 2 can help you make your inner life with God a consistent daily adventure.

Group Dialogue: One of my purposes in this book is to help those who are seeking God's presence in group dialogue. Whether your group is just beginning its spiritual search or is continuing to travel the road of Christian growth, my book is designed for you. One of the "Steps into Silence" in chapter 2 offers special help in relating a group's life and mission to personal meditation. And there are several other ways in which you and your fellow seekers may wish to use these pages.

You may need a way to build dynamic outreach onto your group's already constructed foundation of prayer and Bible study. You may need stimulating discussion starters for a youth group, or a creative way to get an adult study group to move from talk to action. Your group may be looking for direction, a way to find where God would lead you in your pilgrimage with him, with each other and with his world. Or, you may just want to read and discuss, and leave open any possibility of action.

You will find the questions at the end of each chapter especially helpful for group use. Use them according to your group's style, or let them be a springboard to lift your group to new steps forward.

You may be led to start a group (begin with two people, if you like) that commits itself to sharing with each other the contemplative insights and world encounters which come when using this book along with your personal time of meditating. If so, determine that all group members will be fully committed to the group and its growth.

The life that listens is the life that opens itself to others.

Writing Your Own Journal: These pages are for writing, as well as reading. Each chapter concludes with some blank pages. You can thus use this book to record your own thoughts, feelings, and prayers. Before you read a chapter, spend some time thinking about, and feeling into, the "contrasting words" in the title. Prior to your reading turn to the first blank page and write what occurs within you when you focus on those words. After you finish reading the chapter, return to the same blank page. Use it to celebrate any new insights of yourself, or of your relationship with God and the world. As you use this creative space, you will find additional suggestions for your own journaling. Here is a way to tap your own creativity as well as writing your own statements of faith.

Mission Action (for yourself, or your group, or both): As you get in touch with the lively God, he will lead you to mission action. How and where is God calling you to recognize him? In what way does he want to *be* in you, so that part of the world may know him through you? Become aware of God's mission for you. Then, follow where he leads.

As I began to believe that this book could really be, I found myself breathing deeply, with some more refreshment than usual. I could never have been argued into believing how much flexibility and adaptiveness is required for a fully occupied person to write a book. The work convinced me. I sometimes found myself early in the morning in our kitchen, writing on paper plates—the only thing within my grasp when the inspiration hit me. I spent hours of some vacation days at Spring Lodge and Cottages in Cedarville, Michigan, writing, honing, and revising. That in itself was an experience that combined meditation and my life in the world. I was with my family, and the only quiet place I could find was a secluded lagoon hidden behind pine trees, where I sat in a boat, in the silence, enveloped in a spirit of creative inspiration. Somehow, the work was completed.

I have come finally to believe that this book is an outgrowth first of God's will to guide me in the midst of noise, and secondly of my own will to listen, silently, to God. For both of these facts I thank him.

Bill J. Vamos

Elkhart, Indiana

THE LIFE THAT LISTENS

1.

The Life That Listens

John 16:25–33

However else you may feel and think about yourself, it's likely that you are now—or soon will be—a man, or woman, of the world. That phrase affirms your earthly existence. I don't mean that you're planning to sell your soul for the world's fickle rewards. My meaning is simply a description of where you and I live. We circulate in the middle of the pleasure and pain, garbage and glitter with which the world pulsates every day.

You and I want to believe that God can withstand this world, in spite of what it might do to him, and in spite of what the world might do to us. We want to know that there is a God with whom we can communicate wherever we happen to live in the real world.

The working day so often ends with the feeling that you are the long-distance runner who has just finished an exhausting race. You wonder where God is. "How can he be with me, on such a treadmill?"

Or you try to manage the family income. You know you buy some things you shouldn't, but resisting them is beyond you. Somehow, you can't find the few dollars you want to give to your church, or to others who need your help. You want to know if God can help.

Or perhaps death intervenes between you and people you haven't yet had time to really know and love. And you say, "God, can you do anything about my loneliness? I need you."

Is there a God, One we can know, who lives in this world?

That's where we begin the life that listens. Our purpose is frequent meetings with the God who claims this world as his own sacred turf. Our source book is the Bible. Nowhere in literature is there a more worldly book than the Scriptures, if you understand "worldly" to mean God's participation in our earthbound existence.

The Bible Shows Us a "Worldly" God

Ever since God created the world and called it good, he has been involved in every facet of its operation. The Book of Genesis is a commentary on environmental protection, energy conservation, sexuality, family life, the meaning and origin of the city, as well as a history of a nation. Exodus presents the most dramatic story of a human rights movement ever written. The Psalms treat our loneliness with sensitive and profound companionship, all given to a total community. The prophets make politics and economics the chief spiritual issues of the day. The Gospels show us God's way of dealing with our yearning for purpose in life. And Paul presents salvation as the freedom to look at the world through the windows of a new creation. You can summarize the entire biblical message by saying: God and the world belong together.

That may be just the news we need to hear. Today's world is a grim and fearful place. A recent cartoon character in my local newspaper sees it this way: "It used to be that your success was measured by your ability to progress onward and upward, day after day, in your chosen field. Now you're a success if you can just hold on to what you've got."

One night our youngest daughter, Susan, went around the house turning out most of the lights. When she finished she said, "If we save electricity now, we may still have energy when I grow up." That's pretty heavy for one so young. But it's a clue to the seemingly endless perplexities in our contemporary world.

Some time ago, in Chicago, the driver of my cab and I

had an opportunity for a forty-five-minute conversation on our way to O'Hare. I opened with a one-minute statement, and he finished with forty-four minutes of rebuttal—Chicago style. He had had a date with his dentist and I was a convenient target for his disgruntled feelings. But I did learn a lot about what's going on in the world. His conversation reflected today's moods. He lamented: "You know, there's so much change in this world today that I don't feel at home in it any more. It used to be, when a kid robbed the poorbox, the priest would reprimand him for it—I'm a Catholic and that's why I'm telling you this—and then he would find some work for the kid to do, and pay him for the work. Today, if a kid robs the poorbox, the priest calls a policeman, who takes the kid to jail. And another thing," (he kept skipping from one subject to another), "I don't believe in this foreign aid business, either. We have too many people in our own country that we have to care for. Let me tell you the kind of thing I really think is right. Jerry Lewis. Did you see the telethon the other night, when he made $30 million to fight muscular dystrophy? That's the kind of person who really touches my heart."

Well, I couldn't let all of this go by without at least a brief minority report, so I interrupted and said, "Well, tell me this. We in America have more creature comforts than we need, while many other countries don't even have the basic necessities to provide for their people. How do you feel about that? Don't you think we should help them?" He replied, "Yes, I suppose we should. But if we do, those millionaire Arabs better help, too."

On the airplane flying home, I thought about what he had been telling me. He was really saying, "The world is changing so fast it threatens me. It's so impersonal that I don't really feel like I'm part of it any more. And it's driving me to the place where my back is against the wall; I'm having to lean more and more on my instinct for self-preservation."

That's a commentary on our age. And I asked myself: What is it that we fear most as we live in a world that seems to be crying out almost hysterically for sanity and survival? Is it just a lower income that we fear? For many that's a very real concern.

GOD IN A QUAKING WORLD

I believe our universal anxiety is much deeper than that. We fear that our lives are not connected to anything permanent. Our basic struggle today is theological. We feel that we might finally have to ask, "Have I been spending myself in the battle of life for nothing?"

Look at our world: Assassination, bombing, economic turbulence, emotional crippling: all in abundance. Where is hope? Where is meaning? Where is a purpose for life that is reliable?

Our reaction has been to withdraw. To scurry to a place of personal safety and stay there. The religions that are flourishing today are those which promise to deal with your inner construction by providing you with a sacred insulation, so that the wintry winds of the world's change and depression won't affect your inner temperature.

But that is not where we meet God. Nowhere in the Bible do we find God leading people to a permanent escape hatch. Instead, what we discover is a God who shows people how to move forward when the only clear path seems to lie behind them.

Can you believe that? It sounds incredible, until you realize that it really is in a broken and destructive world that we encounter the God who comes to heal and to recreate. In John 16, Jesus tells the disciples that they are approaching a moment of heavy darkness. It will envelop them and him. His final day is drawing near. He has also told them that there is a time yet to come when they will feel closer to him than ever before.

And in verse 29, he makes clear to them what had previously been hidden. He says, "I came from the Father and have come into the world." Notice: not into a sanctuary of isolation, but into the vortex of our human struggle. Again, "I am leaving the world and going to the Father." Not only does Jesus bring God into the world, he gathers the world into his arms and returns it to God. His disciples respond, "Ah, now you are speaking plainly, not in any figure" (v. 29). For the first time they saw, felt, and clearly understood the living bridge built by Jesus between God and the world. It was as though a shaft of light had broken through the clouds which had obscured their minds.

It could well be that we, the people of the late twentieth century, are also ready for such a breakthrough. It could be that we can see God today in a way we couldn't manage in the past. In John 16, Jesus is shown preparing for his crucifixion. And his pilgrimage provides the supreme example of the creativity to be found in human chaos and suffering.

GOD LIVES IN A DYING WORLD

Between the fifth and sixth games of a recent World Series, a newspaper reported an experience of Sparky Anderson, then manager of the Cincinnati Reds. Sparky had attempted to win the World Series twice before and failed, but winning it this time was not nearly so important to him as it once had been. The reason for his changed outlook was a friend named Milton Blish, who lived in Southern California. Sparky had discovered, through a letter from a friend, that Milton had cancer, and was given about eight weeks to live. Every day during the play-offs and the Series, Sparky Anderson called Milton to ask him how he was getting along, and to tell him he was thinking of him. To the reporter who was interviewing him, he said, "Somehow, winning the world championship doesn't have the intense attraction that it once had for me. Now I see what life means in a deeper dimension. Now I've somehow discovered what is really there. And win or lose, there's a new peace in me." At a time when Sparky needed help, Milton had given Sparky a job. Sparky never forgot his kindness. Calling his friend day after day enabled him to look into life's deepest realities.

Let's put that into the context of our world situation. We do meet God in a dying world—because we are ready and able to meet him there. You may say, "Well, I recognize that some of the time. But for a good bit of my life, that sort of thinking becomes very obscure. You know, I fall apart rather easily these days."

Don't you think God is prepared for us to fall apart? Look at John 16:31. (Remember that the disciples have just said, "Lord, it was a breakthrough. We understand more clearly than ever before.") Jesus then goes on to say, "Do you now believe? The hour is coming, indeed, it is come, when you will be scattered, every man [person] to his home, and will leave me alone." You're going to desert me.

It's to a failing people that a crucified and risen God comes. In fact, Jesus carefully points to his followers' failure. He wants them to trust him even when they are utterly ashamed of themselves. Look at verse 33: "I've said this to you that in me you may have peace." I want you to know that when you're utterly disillusioned about yourselves, when you can't trust yourselves any more, I still believe in you. And at the end of verse 33, Jesus makes a startling claim. He says, "In the world you have tribulation, but be of good cheer. I have overcome the world."

Think about the conditions under which he made that statement. He stands on the threshold of death—facing the desertion of his followers—alone—even beginning to feel abandoned by his Father, and he says to his people: "You're going to have trouble in this world, but courage: I have conquered the world." That's faith.

INVITATION TO MEDITATION

That's where our faith is today. And that is where our mission is. As you move into this study guide, I invite you to look at the world around you. Listen for the sound of God rustling in the winds that both calm you and toss you about. These chapters are meant to lead you to a rocklike strength within, so that you may face the storms without. But mind you, I'm not writing prescriptions for spiritual numbness. Indeed, these contemplations may well usher into your life some new struggles you haven't faced before, such as: Where do my life's priorities and my faith in God meet? What is the connection between what I see on my daily schedule, and a God of peace and love? And where is God in the corporate structures of this world, that at once oppress people and are so life-giving?

Be a partner with me in the life that listens. On the first blank page at the end of this chapter write "Noise" and "Silence." Then write—or think about—what those words mean to you.

These are the concepts with which we will deal in the next chapter. For now, think about those words, and today—or sometime soon—find a quiet place that's right for you to meditate. Feel and sense and think about what those words say and do to you. Gather your faith and focus it in relation to those words. As you do, you may discover God.

It's certain that he's waiting.

(This space is yours! Use it for writing your own journal. Try using my suggestion at the end of chapter 1. Use any remaining space on these two journal pages for the flow of your own ideas. The "Questions for Meditation and Discussion" which follow the second blank page can be helpful. Perhaps you will want to write a prayer, or begin to make some jottings about how this workbook can best meet your needs.)

QUESTIONS FOR MEDITATION OR GROUP DIALOGUE

1. Where do you meet God? Is it always in a worship service? Is it ever with your family? Or, in a world crisis or some good news about world affairs? Do you meet God in other people? Or, when you are alone?
2. How do you *feel* about God? Is he a Companion for you, or an anonymous deity? Does he threaten you, or inspire you?
3. The cab driver said: "The world is . . . so impersonal that I don't feel like I'm part of it any more." Do you share his feeling?
4. Jesus is ". . . the supreme example of the creativity to be found in human chaos and suffering." Do you believe such realities can be creative? Have you known God in adversity?
5. Jesus wants us to trust him even when we are ashamed of ourselves. Are you willing to do that? Is it good news to you?
6. Ask yourself: Do I know the Spirit of God *within me?*
7. What is the connection between your faith in God and the priorities by which you live?

2.

Noise and Silence

Psalm 46; Psalm 95

When I look at the words "noise" and "silence," my first thought is: we live in a noise-addicted world. That thought came home to me very vividly when I read a recent newspaper account about an enterprising salesman who realized that each time he drove through a highway tunnel in Fort Lauderdale, Florida, the tunnel shut off his radio.

There was only silence in his car. On the conviction that people would prefer any kind of noise instead of silence, he's had the tunnel wired so that commercials and public service announcements are constantly broadcast, and heard by anyone whose radio is turned on. The only way you can escape that noise is to turn off your radio.

That's a symptom of the age in which we live.

I'm reminded of a cartoon. Mother is driving home with her four small children, the family dog, and several bags of groceries. On her face you can see a combination of tension, frustration, anger, and near hysteria, as the steering wheel begins to vibrate under her ever-tightening grip. Behind her all four small children are talking at the same time. Listen to the conversation behind her:

"Tell Billy to stop waving at the car behind us."

"Daddy's good hat is back here, and Dolly's standing on it!"

"Which bag are the lollipops in?"

"Blow your horn and make that police car get out of the way, Mom."

"Janie just dropped the ketchup bottle in on top of the prune juice, and the bag's leaking."

"Drive faster, we're missing a good program on TV."

"Stop bouncing the car, I can't read the message on the cereal box."

"It's cold back here, sitting on this frozen food."

"Who put the fingerprints on the back window?"

"Why'd you turn the radio off?"

"Jimmy's opening the cookie bag."

"You don't smile very much when you drive, do you, Mommy?"

DEFINITIONS OF NOISE (AND SOUND)

Recently, I asked some friends to define what was noisy in their lives. Here are some of their answers:

"Oh, that alarm clock in the morning."

"News reporting and news on television."

"The intensity of communication today is noise. Our problem isn't so much a lack of communicating, as it is overcommunicating."

"Faces scream noise. Sometimes people don't say anything verbally, but their faces shriek at you."

A businessman said, "Sometimes I read noise in memorandums."

"The internal noises are the most difficult."

I asked these same friends to make a distinction between sound and noise. Listen to some of the responses:

"What can be more joyful than the sound of happy children playing? Or fans rooting for the winning team at a ball game? Or your favorite kind of music? Those are sounds."

A teenage girl said: "When my brothers are upstairs screaming and yelling, that's noise. When they're upstairs playing a game, that's sound."

"Stravinsky is noise; Mozart is sound." (Depending, of course, on your tastes.)

There *is* a difference between noise and sound.

For most people, today's world is noisy. Good sound is frequently overshadowed by an avalanche of noise.

Then noise becomes a clamorous assault. So much so that in our day many of us yearn for silence. For many people in our technological age, the comment, "If I could only find some peace and quiet in this house," is typical. That's not true for everyone. For some persons, there's too much silence. People who live alone will often say, "I'd like to have more sound. In fact, I'd like to have more noise in my life."

SILENCE IS NOT ALWAYS SERENE

Yet when quiet is available, most of us have trouble handling it creatively. Silence and serenity are not automatic companions. One person reflected on that truth by saying, "Silence takes me back to the beginning of time. In the beginning, nothing was there. There was only darkness. It was very still; but it wasn't a pleasant stillness. My feelings are that it was a lonely time. God must have felt that way, because as he created the world, he began speaking. And he brought forth sound, with which we associate—birds singing, wind blowing, the rivers flowing. There was still a sort of lonely hush over it all. Then God put human beings on this earth. At first it was beautiful, but you know the story of Adam and Eve. To me, this is where the noise began."

There are contemporary illustrations of what we could call noisy silence. For instance, there is the void that comes when one person gives another person the "silent treatment" as a strategy of angry attack. Or there is the tension that comes when people at a party become reserved and quiet.

The potential discord of silence was once explained to me: "Silence takes us away from the opportunity to structure time. Silence becomes a threat because it's unstructured. We want to have some noise going on all the time. It's as though we need that hummer in the background. Yet at the same time, we hunger for some depth and serenity in quietude. Today we're searching for healing quietness."

YOU CAN DEVELOP CONTEMPLATIVE SILENCE

Our faith tells us that we can develop contemplative silence, which is far more than just the absence of sound. Such silence moves beyond quieting the outer and inner stimuli, and moves us to touching God.

The writer of Psalm 46 speaks of that kind of tranquility when he says, "Be still, and know that I am God." Before that, he speaks of the earth changing, and the mountains shaking in the heart of the sea, and the waters roaring and foaming. He reflects on his era, a time of imminent war. But he looks beyond the current catastrophe to an even greater turbulence. He goes back to the primeval chaos before creation. He looks ahead to the final days of the future. He says, "Suppose the very earth moves off its foundation. Suppose that the oceans erupt over the earth. The Lord of Hosts will continue to be our God. So, God says, 'Be still.'" (Some scholars translate the Hebrew word as "relax"; others translate it, "leave off from waging war, and know that I am God.")

We need the power of our faith to create times of quietness. Thomas Kelly described that renewing silence when he said, "There is within us all a holy, infinite Center, a Life, Who speaks in us and through us to the world. We've all heard this Holy Whisper at times. At times we've followed that Holy Whisper. And an amazing equilibrium of life, an amazing effectiveness of living, set in."[1]

A friend who recently attended a group retreat devoted to contemplative silence reflected that reality when he said, "I realized that in those seventeen hours of silence I could use quiet as a way of reaching God in a far deeper manner than I've ever known before. When I go home to relax, I sit down and I turn on the television set, which is one noise drowning out another, even though it's different than the noise I hear all day. The silence on that retreat was a combination of serenity and power at the same time."

That was a communal experience, which has a special kind of redemptive strength (I highly recommend a silent retreat led by an experienced person as a good introduction into the Silence). But every one of us has the opportunity when we're alone to use silence creatively. How? I'm going to list some suggestions.

We'll call them "Steps into Silence." But first a word of caution. You may initially feel that the process I've outlined is too demanding—above all, don't charge into this like a conqueror about to seize a throne. Walk slowly, quietly, a short way each day, with your heart and hands open to receive God's nearness. My own experience shows that, once I lived into the process and became acquainted with its power and Good News, I could let God guide me. Remember, God is the Silence. And be careful to use these guidelines as a help for yourself, making sure you don't press yourself for perfection. God welcomes your efforts, and he will help.

Step #1: Claim Your Own Time and a Relaxed Place

Decide on a daily module of time. Many people find that the same time period each day is essential. Some can be flexible.

Start with five minutes per day, if that is an honest beginning for you. *You* decide how long your devotional time will be at the outset. You should work up a plan that moves toward an hour each day. Do whatever is achievable for you. At first, five minutes may drag by, but trust that your spiritual hunger will increase. You may want even more than an hour after you begin to taste God's nourishment for the inner you. If you make this process Priority One, it will work for you.

You will also find it necessary to claim your own devotional place, one with the most noiseless circumstances possible. This may be your most difficult step, but it is worth the effort. You may need to ask tolerance or help from your family or co-workers. Your daily schedule may require a variation in the place of prayer. That will work, too, but be sure to have a spiritual home base.

It is essential to have a place where you can relax. I find it helpful to let go of my body tension. That process enhances inner quiet. If by chance, some unexpected outside noises occasionally draw near, ask God to help you screen them out. I also remind myself that, in Silence, I can quiet my inner noise and move beyond my thoughts and feelings to actually be in touch with God. I let my body become peaceful, letting all of its parts join in this time of listening to God in calmness. You might even fall asleep while you are doing that. You can thank God for that, since such sleep may be an ideal form of worship.

As you enter the Silence, pray this prayer: *Lord Jesus, come into my mind, my body, my feelings, my spirit. Forgive me and make me whole.*

Step #2: Listen to God's Presence and Respond

The chapters in this book can be an aid to your devotions. Before you read each of the remaining chapters, reflect on the contrasting words in each of the chapter headings. Then move through each chapter at a steady yet unhurried pace, making sure to contemplate the Scripture on which it is based.

When you have finished your reading of each chapter, reflect on the companion questions that are provided.*

Throughout this process, use the two blank pages following the chapter as your own journal. This workbook will more effectively increase your spiritual depth if you let it help you give expression to the life of your spirit. On the top of the first blank page, I have given specific suggestions for the use of your journaling pages. Here is an opportunity to do your own writing.

Step #3: Pray:

Use Adoration,
    Thanksgiving,
        Confession and Assurance of Forgiveness,
            Prayers for Others,
                Prayers for Yourself.

(You may want to reverse steps 2 and 3 from time to time. You may prefer to use only one of these steps at the beginning. If so, include the next step as soon as you can.)

Step #4: Make a Commitment and Be Accountable

Make a definite commitment to grow your daily devotional discipline. We are not naturally inclined to listen to God. If we don't receive instant inspiration, we easily become impatient and drop the process. I believe I am like many other people, able to open the treasure of daily solitude with God when I voluntarily make myself accountable to another person, as well as to my own self-discipline. It's a combination of realistic self-knowledge and trust in the power of Christian community.

*For additional help beyond this book, see Thomas Kelly's *Testament of Devotion*, and the devotional writings of Thomas Merton, Henri Nouwen, and Elizabeth O'Connor.

Ask God to guide you to a spiritual partner. Your friend may already have learned a discipline of daily devotions. If not, develop the possibility of each of you nurturing your individual time for listening to God. Be accountable to each other. Resolve to be consistent in holding the other person to the specific commitment he or she has made. Combine gentleness toward the struggle of personal growth, with no-nonsense objectivity.

Here is the point where personal meditation and group dialogue can come together. Personal accountability can be more readily achievable when we root it in the life of a group. If possible, let the personal meditation commitment be an individual discipline accepted by each person in your group.

Either choose spiritual partners within your group, or let three group members be the group's spiritual helpers. The others in the group can each be accountable to one of these three persons. And each of them can be accountable to one of their own number.

In this way you can share with others the growth and frustration of your own devotional life, and your group can deepen a corporate life that both listens and leads.

SILENCE LEADS TO MISSION

If you attempt this kind of discipline, you can put yourself in touch with God's "sound of silence." But that's not the conclusion of your inner pilgrimage. Relaxing in contemplative silence enables you to perceive God and to proclaim his presence in noise. When you are quiet in God's presence, you become more able to speak for him in the presence of people. That's the pattern Jesus followed. Who spent more time going apart by himself to commune with God than Jesus? But at the same time, who was more in touch with the world and with people than Jesus Christ?

The witness of Christian contemplatives throughout history is that our contact with God in meditation gives us greater power for Christ in the world. It *is* possible to learn how to transform the cacophony of contemporary noise into that "joyful noise unto God" of which the writer of Psalm 95 spoke.

Another friend recently shared with me her innovative system of using quiet to reach God in the midst of noise. She said, "Sometimes I feel that I'm in desperate need to pray to God, yet I'm surrounded by noise and mass confusion. So I steal away within myself. I get my mind on one track and there is within me silence. Then I allow myself to get in touch with God through an inner prayer. I gather strength from this prayer to go back into the noise and chaos with a different outlook and a better understanding." Someone said to this person, "How do you ever manage that?" She said, "Well, I guess the reason I developed this life style is because my need for it was so great." Perhaps the church can learn to develop that same capacity in other people with the same need.

But we also need to make quiet possible for all the people in our urbanized society who are bombarded with noise. It's not just a matter of enabling people to cope with noise. As Christians, our mission includes reducing the decibel level that exists in this world.

Recently the Environmental Protection Agency said that there were at least 35 million Americans who never escape noise. Most of these people live in the inner cities of our nation. Dr. Ernest A. Peterson of the University of Miami School of Medicine has said that there's an enormous overlay of environmental and physiological factors in hypertension, and noise may be an important factor. Which says something about the wisdom of the supersonic transport landing in New York City—or anywhere else.

And it tells us something about the mission of Christ's church in the world, which heretofore we may not have considered.

The issue about noise and silence is not, "Do they please me?" The issue is, "How do I use both as avenues by which God may reach into my being, through either tranquility or disturbance?" The key to discovering God's staying power in a helter-skelter world is to use silence as a reservoir for the flow of the grace of God from us into the world.

A contemplative person I know shared with me a recent entry in his spiritual journal. He said, "There's nothing like the refreshing power of quietude. It rebuilds me from within, and redirects my life. I trust God, again, and look for him in the midst of the world. In the Silence, God sets me free from being controlled by pressures and disappointments. I can live in the world, but not of it."

That's what it means to be still—and know—that God is with you.

*Use this space to reflect on the message of chapter 2 for you. Use the Questions for Meditation or Group Dialogue.
*Quietly contemplate the Scriptures for this chapter, Psalms 46 and 95.

.

.

QUESTIONS FOR MEDITATION OR GROUP DIALOGUE

1. From your own observations and experience would you agree that "... we live in a noise-addicted world"? Are there any times of silence in your life?
2. What is *noisy* to you? What are some of your favorite *sounds*? Have you thought about the needs of people for whom there is too much silence?
3. "Silence and serenity are not automatic companions." When does silence feel heavy to you? Is silence threatening because it takes away that protective "hummer in the background"? If so, why?
4. Does the experience of knowing a refreshing quietness appeal to you? Do you feel that your Christian growth and your own need for renewal would benefit from creative silence?
5. If you are not using a devotional discipline, or feel you need new life in your personal worship, consider making a commitment to the "Steps into Silence." If your current devotional life is meaningful, what are some of its gifts that you would like to celebrate and sustain?
6. The church's mission today includes reducing the noise level that reverberates across the world. Can you think of ways that will help to accomplish this?

3.

Alone and Belonging

Ephesians 3:17–19; 2 Corinthians 4:8, 9

Once upon a time, the pastor of a church invited those in his audience who were not yet members to join the church—to belong. A woman who heard the sermon responded after worship by grasping the pastor's hands, looking at him with tears in her eyes, and saying, "Pastor, I want to belong. I want to belong."

Every one of us feels that same yearning. We want to belong.

But don't most of us live overcrowded and hyper-socialized lives? In the words made famous by Greta Garbo, we sigh heavily, "I vant to be alone."

We readily agree with Marshall McLuhan's comment that mass transit will never work in the United States because "a person's car is the only place he can be alone and think."

Alone and belonging. Those words describe two of our basic human needs. Like most of our deeper feelings, they lead to plus and minus factors in our lives. Both being alone and belonging can be creative, and both can be destructive.

When alone equals privacy, it can be a delight.

When you are alone in isolation, it can be bitter.

When belonging is the tenderness you can win or lose by the caprice of the group, it can devastate you.

But when belonging is the solid and immovable bond of friendship, it lifts you.

"Alone-ness"—Blessing and Curse

Think about your own human experience. Consider the times when you're alone. Haven't you been by yourself and loved it? And haven't you had other moments when your insides literally screamed for companionship?

An artist in our church made this comment about alone-ness: "Last week, I had three whole days alone at my drawing board. It was delicious. Those days were so full." She was alone with her creative living space—alone with her inspiration. But if she had been a commercial artist with a deadline at the end of those three days, being alone at that drawing board might have given her those clammy, solitary feelings that need no help to produce indigestion.

And if she didn't meet the deadline, she had better have a good sense of "belonging" with her employer.

As a seasoned pastor, I leap at the opportunities for privacy to meditate, to study, or to pray. Just plain solitude would be welcome. But I remember my service as a student pastor to a rural parish for four months when I lived in a ten-room manse—all alone. Much of the time I felt as if I was in solitary confinement. I couldn't wait to get home for two or three days of tender, loving care.

If you attempt to coordinate a family, you may find that even your car is stuffed with people. And you would do most anything for time to call your own. But if you live in a nursing home, even the sound of footsteps in the hallway is reassuring. You ache for visits from other people. Being alone is not a delicious choice for everyone in our society. Solitude is positive when it means creative seclusion. When it is a wall of separation, it hurts.

Belonging: Also Blessing and Curse

The same is true of belonging. There is a belonging which means no more than temporary approval. It comes and goes with the whims of a fickle society. But there is also a belonging that authentically includes you.

A member of our church told me of a recent visit to an elementary school, for an open house. While she was there, she noticed several pictures on the bulletin board.

One of them caught her eye. The student had drawn a picture of a basketball player who was about 6'11". He was holding on his shoulders another boy who was about 5'2". The short boy on top of the tall boy's shoulders was stuffing the ball through the basket. And underneath in bold letters was the caption: "Friendship." The person who told me this said, "I didn't know which of the two boys drew the picture, but it really didn't matter. That is belonging."

On the other hand, our society seems to be surfeited with a togetherness that is very empty to us. David Belgum tells of a young small-town girl who traveled to freshman orientation week at a Midwestern university with two friends from her own community. She didn't see them once during that entire week. She had people around her most of the time, but she had no opportunity to be with her friends. Her most perplexing experience was at mealtime. She and her friends ate in the same cafeteria, which served 1600 people. There were 800 in line A, going in one direction, and 800 in line B, going in the opposite direction. Her student identification number was #306–72. Her friends had identification numbers beginning with #102 and 104, but she couldn't reach them in the cafeteria line. Every moment she had togetherness, but no friendship.[1]

There's a vast difference between surface belonging and the bond of friendship. There are lively churches which have a theology of permanent inclusion, like the church in which E. Stanley Jones grew up. He said, "I don't think I would have survived as a young person if it hadn't been for my church. When I rejoiced, they rejoiced with me. When I was weak, they strengthened me. And once when I had a rather bad fall, they gathered around me by love and prayer, and without condemnation or censure, lovingly lifted me back to my feet again."

But there are also churches that provide only superficial togetherness. They are a group wherein you only play a role. You're a deacon or an elder or a trustee—or a choir member or a pew sitter or a pastor. When can you be a person? Belonging is beautiful when your relatedness creates dependable friendship. When it is no more than cosmetic togetherness, belonging can be ugly, almost devastating.

GOD SAYS, "I BELONG TO YOU; YOU BELONG TO ME"

How does a person make it in this existential paradox? *Is* there a way to manage being alone *and* belonging, when we know such experiences can be both phony and real?

The biblical faith unscrambles this living riddle for us by showing us that our problem is fear of being left out. We can handle being alone and fellowship with a very shaky perspective, because we never know when family, corporation, union, classmates, or colleagues, will write us off. We will do almost anything to keep from being rejected. And that's where biblical faith comes through—with insight and support. In the Bible we discover a God who will do almost anything to tell us we are never negated.

Writing in Ephesians 3:17–19, Paul shows us the meaning of God's inclusiveness. Paul had done everything possible to resist Jesus, the risen Christ, but he was finally captured by him—a captivity that released Paul from the prison of anticipated rejection. In Jesus he discovered a link with God—a belonging—that could never be broken. He wraps up his whole theology in the words: "I pray that you . . . together with all God's people, may have the power to understand how broad and long, how high and deep is Christ's love. Yes, may you come to know his love . . . and be so completely filled with the perfect fulness of God" (TEV). Here is spiritual energy to be alone, and to belong, even when those experiences come with vague and shadowy dimensions.

Not too long ago I heard God communicating that message to me. The message is beginning to release me from a self-imposed prison of isolation. I spent a week with a group of nine other people in a "Wellspring Workshop," sponsored by The Church of the Saviour, in Washington, D.C. We began with two days of silent retreat, moved to workshops on anger, sexuality, and gift-evoking, and concluded the week digging garbage out of a totally neglected airshaft in an inner-city apartment building, celebrating and worshiping.

Before the celebration I walked out on the shakiest spiritual limb I've ever been on in my life. Somehow, slogging through five years' residue of broken glass, diapers and despair in that airshaft connected me with some rubbish inside myself. I'd been feeling on the fringe of the group all week, attempting to impress them with my position as Senior Pastor of First Presbyterian Church, my poetic and preacherly prowess, and my dedicated piety. They tolerated my efforts and endured the barriers I was establishing with them by huckstering my image. On Saturday evening, when we returned from inner-city Washington, I had an irresistible, frightening urge to tell them something, and I wasn't quite sure what it was or how to say it. So I simply blurted out, through tears and many more words than it takes to write the truth on this page, "I need you to love me. Not my image. Not my achievements. Not my professional capacity—just me. All my life I've been afraid that I won't be loved unless what I do is perfect (not just good or acceptable, but supreme). And somehow, I can't endure life in this group (or in this world) any longer without admitting that."

What a relief! I cried more tears (something I thought it unmanly to do) in that hour and a half than I have in any previous five years in my life. They were tears of anger and release, and then of joy. The people in the group gave me their gifts of support—all the way from hugs of encouragement to "tough love" comments that hit home with a jolt. And I started to discover within me (in the language of transactional analysis) a "spontaneous child" who likes to dance, and sing, and laugh, and smile, more deeply than I ever have before. In the last two days of our week together, the orderly, disciplined, erudite Senior Pastor of First Presbyterian Church received from the group the nickname, "Raggedy Andy."

It's not all heavenly for me. It scares me with a whole new growth process (which I also welcome with delight). But it's a new freedom to belong, not as a functionary, but as my own self.

It came *through* disciplined times of silence with God and the support of a loving group. But the Giver is an old and new Friend who calls himself Alpha and Omega, Beginning and End: the Living God.

If I don't do anything else for you with this book, please hear me echoing to you the message I'm hearing God speak to me: "I have called you by name" (Isa. 43:1, NEB). God is saying, "I am wholly yours and you are wholly mine."

Knowing that, you and I can be alone, and uncover creative privacy, no matter what our circumstances may be. Whatever happens in our lives, you and I are going to spend some of our days alone. Sometimes that will be an adventure, and sometimes it will hurt. But when we know that God wants us, we can make those experiences times of belonging.

J. Middleton Murry reports an experience familiar to many. Sorrow and despair had brought him near to suicide. But in that moment of ultimate loneliness, something happened. Murry describes it this way: "What happened then? If I could tell that, I should tell a secret indeed. But a moment came when the darkness of the ocean changed into light, the cold into warmth. When it bathed me and I was renewed. When it swept in one great wave over the shores and frontiers of myself. When the room was filled with a Presence, and I knew I was not alone. That I would never be alone any more. That the universe beyond held no menace, for I was part of it. That in some way for which I had sought in vain so many years, I belonged. And because I belonged, I was no longer I, but something different, which could never be afraid in the old ways. Or cowardly with the old cowardice."[2]

I've never read a more profound description of belonging—and yet it happened when Murry was alone.

Our need is to be alone while we belong. The ultimate answer to that singular need is God's unwavering reliability. Because of that reliability, we can become open to other people, and to ourselves, even in a world that buffets us with the winds of ominous change. God reaches us with resilient companionship when we're alone—and when we're together.

Paul shared an inner affirmation that he knew he would never lose when he wrote to the Corinthians: "We are handicapped on all sides, but we are never frustrated. We are puzzled, but never in despair. We are persecuted, but we never have to stand it alone. We may be knocked down, but we are never knocked out" (2 Cor. 4:8, 9, Phillips).

When you let God fill you with that kind of affirming grace, you can be alone and belong at the same time—and no one can take it from you.

Consider "Alone" and "Belonging" in your own life.
Reflect on chapter 3 and the questions that follow these journal pages.
Meditate on the Scriptures for chapter 3, Ephesians 3:17–19 and 2 Corinthians 4:8, 9. Put yourself into the history, the setting, and the people involved. What is God saying to you? What do you want to say to him?

QUESTIONS FOR MEDITATION OR GROUP DIALOGUE

1. Evaluate your own times of being alone. Are they joyous? Or dismal? Or sometimes one, and sometimes the other? Use the same evaluation with your experiences of belonging.
2. Does your church offer people authentic belonging? Does it have a life together in which people can lean on each other, and support one another with caring? Would you call your church, "my family," and would you go to some of its people when your life "... is fractured and needs mending"? If not, what is God calling you to do in your congregation to nurture a community of trust and openness?
3. Our problem with being alone and with belonging is fear of rejection. In Christ Jesus we discover a link with God that can never be broken. Do you know God as One who says to you: "I am wholly yours and you are wholly mine"?
4. Is the presence of God real to you? Can you say: "God is *with* me. God is *with* others"?
5. What can you do to bring God's companionship to other people?

4.

Work and Play

Genesis 1:26–2:7; Mark 10:13–16

Framed in a drugstore in Beverley, Massachusetts, are the following work rules from the year 1854:

—Store will open promptly at 6:00 a.m., and remain open until 9:00 p.m. year round.

—Store will not be open on the Sabbath unless absolutely necessary, and then only for a few minutes.

—Any employee who is in the habit of smoking Spanish cigars, getting shaved at a barbershop, going to dances and other places of amusement, will most surely give his employer reason to suspect his integrity and all-round honesty.

—Each employee must attend Sunday School every week. Male employees are given one evening a week for courting purposes, and two if they go to prayer meeting regularly.

—After fourteen hours of work in the store, the remaining leisure time must be spent in reading good literature.[1]

After I read those rules from a former era, I thought: *We could use the discipline they imply in our haphazard and unbridled society.* But those ancient admonitions also create an image of work and play as repressive "shoulds" and "oughts"—the kind of experience you want to escape by sneaking behind the drugstore for a forbidden game of hide and seek. When work and play are seen only as weighty obligations, they stifle the spirit of a man or a woman, a girl or a boy—and they drive us farther from God.

But there is yet another role for both labor and leisure.

Work and play can be the liberators of the best that is within us.

SOMETIMES WORK IS DRUDGERY

We all know that work can be drudgery. How often we have said: "There just aren't enough hours in the day." "Will I ever be glad when this week is over!" "T.G.I.F.—Thank God, it's Friday!"

Some people dread their work because it bores them. Charles Elliot, the president of Harvard University, once admitted that after some years as president, he no longer found any novelty or fresh interest in his work. He went so far as to say that nine-tenths of the time his job was sheer routine, dull and monotonous.

Genesis 3 tells us that at the beginning of the world's life, work was designated a curse. Work is not negative by nature; it becomes negative when we try to take the world in which we work out of God's hands and make it exclusively our own. In our greed we relegate to the poor the empty pursuit of laboring just to maintain poverty. Many people make their work nothing more than a tension-filled ego trip. Such work can be an anchor that drags you down.

EVEN PLAY CAN BE BURDENSOME

Play can also be drudgery. William Stringfellow says that we're not likely to find relief from the burden of work in the leisure of our present day. These days, leisure is often hyperorganized for the sake of filling time. Stringfellow points to the way people will use every free moment day and night to sit hypnotically, in an addicted stupor, before the television set. "Leisure has become the commercial exploitation of boredom."[2]

And play, like work, can drive us farther from God. Exodus tells the story of the people of Israel and the golden calf. The people had become impatient with Moses, and with the God who Moses had said would lead them to the Promised Land. They convinced Aaron to fashion for them a god of their own making, a calf made of gold. Then the Scripture says: ". . . the people sat down to eat and drink, and they rose up to play" (v. 6). They congratulated themselves on their craftiness by playing bombastic games in front of the god whom *they* had created in their image. But they found that such play could be a debilitating and alienating experience.

CAN WORK AND PLAY BE CREATIVE?

However, there are other possibilities for both work and play—possibilities made glorious and inviting by a redemptive and creative God who also works and plays.

In Mark 10:13–17, Jesus shows us how we can renew our times of toil and our recreation. Look at the Scripture's poignant story: "And they were bringing children to him, that he might touch them, and the disciples rebuked them." (I can almost see the disciples coming in and saying, "Don't bother the Lord. He's busy saving people. Get those children out of here!")

And Jesus becomes furious: "When Jesus saw it, he was indignant, and said to them, 'Let the children come to me. Do not hinder them'" (Mark 10:14a). He was saying in effect, don't stand in their way! The next statement is startling: "For to such belong the kingdom of God. Truly I say to you, whoever does not receive the kingdom of God like a child shall not inherit it" (Mark 10:14b, 15). If you aren't willing to be receptive—if you won't be dependent on the One who loves you, you can't receive the kingdom of God. "And he took them up into his arms, and laid his hands upon them and blessed them" (Mark 10:16).

That suggests a way to make both work and play re-creative experiences. Receive the kingdom of God like a child! Do your work as one laboring in the service of a God who is a mature and trusting Friend. Play like a child—spontaneously frolicking and laughing; finally falling asleep in the arms of your Father-God.

Isn't that an idyllic dream? But how do we make it real? What do you do about the quotas you have to reach every month? Or the pushes and pulls that pressure you in every direction on your job? Moreover, what about those subtle manipulations that push you toward conformity?

We could begin by generating a new attitude toward labor and leisure. When Jesus came, he introduced us to a God who works and plays even in a world that seems to deny his very existence. That's what the phrase "kingdom of God" means. God in Christ is head of the world (not just the Church, but the world)—even though we try unsuccessfully to shut him out.

GOD'S WORK: RELATIONSHIPS

Let yourself see God in your work. Begin by realizing that God works. Genesis 2 shows us a God who is at work at the very beginning of the world. "And on the seventh day God finished his work which he had done, and he rested . . . from all his work which he had done in creation" (vv. 2, 3). Later, when God decides to personally reveal himself to us, he comes as a Person with a job to do. At the outset of Jesus' ministry the question is asked about him: "Is not this the carpenter?" (Mark 6:13). Jesus finds oneness with God in the work that he does: "My Father goes on working and so do I" (John 5:17). Throughout the Scriptures we see a God at work building and rebuilding the world, sometimes in ways that seem very humble. That means that you and I can find God in the work we do. Reuel Howe says that when you talk with people about the Christian gospel and work, begin by affirming the places where you already see God at work with them. Don't tell them about the places where God is not. They're already painfully aware of his absence. Speak with them about the places where God is clearly seen.

A member of our congregation once told me that she meets God in an effort to be open to conversation with the repair and service people who come to her home from time to time. She said, "You'd be amazed at their response to someone who's interested in them; to the opportunity to share a little bit of themselves. And sometimes they provide profound insights. My husband says our repair bills are double because of my efforts, but it's my way of making a pilgrimage with the Holy Spirit."

Another member of our congregation, a businessman, told me that he sees work as an activity that equalizes people. He says, "I walk from my office and go through the factory and see a person sweeping the flooor, and I say to myself, 'That man is the one who makes it all happen. He is a very significant person in this corporation. Just as significant as I. He isn't a drill press, or a wastebasket. He's a human being.' In him I meet God."

Another man tells me that God confronts him when he brings his Christian perspective to the selling process. He says: "Often I will tell a customer not to buy an item in this quarter, because it's going to cost less in the next quarter. That makes fewer dollars for me, but I see it as part of my style as a Christian."

A few corporations do work hard to make God visible in what they do. At least one has given its retail dealers the opportunity to take all of the money they make over a certain level of profit, and give it to charity. Hundreds of thousands of dollars are being given by employees in that corporation because they see God in their productive activity.

God's Work: Justice

The kingdom of God perfuses the work that we do. When you see that, it brings not only refreshing perception, it brings new demands. It brings the judgment of God upon us as well, and calls us to be far more open to his presence in the working world.

The November 1, 1975, issue of *Saturday Review* devoted itself entirely to the theme, " 'Watergating' on Main Street." It says in part: "Watergate was only the tip of the iceberg. The issues of corruption and of distorted values reach deeply into the daily arts and artifices by which we live."[3] When we see work under the grace and power of God, we raise the issue of ethics—professional, corporate, and labor.

We need a new revolution in America—one which transforms the concept that monetary profit, whether personal or corporate, is everything. Roger Shinn gives an illustration: "Sometimes the American people, moved by a combination of self-interest and good will, have tried to help another country suffering from poverty. Churches and other voluntary agencies have sent people and money. Congress, with its usual reluctance, has voted economic aid. The Peace Corps has given educational and engineering help. Everybody regarded these as ethical acts. But while all this was going on, a change. . . . in the prices of [imported goods] did more harm to the economy than all the efforts to help it. Nobody regarded the price change as an ethical issue. . . ."[4]

When you see your work as part of the kingdom of God, it raises a whole host of new questions. For example, wouldn't it be renewing if the people who supervise were to identify more closely with those under their supervision? What would happen if the school superintendent taught in the classroom one week each semester? Let's say, second grade the first semester, and senior high social studies the second semester. What would happen if a union president would work on the assembly line, not just once in his career, but for two weeks every year; or, if a corporation president, as part of his annual activity, were to work as an unskilled laborer in one of the plants? What would happen if a pastor actually stood in the working shoes of his parishioners? And we could reverse the process. Put the parishioners in the pastor's shoes, and the laborers in the president's shoes. If we did that, it could create major redemptive changes in the structure of our work. When you receive the kingdom of God like a child, grace and justice come inevitably together.

GOD PLAYS, TOO

We also see God in our play. Once again, we can begin by recognizing that God plays. That's in the creation story, too. Alexander Miller tells us: "The primeval account of Adam and Eve in the plenitude of created and creative power. . . . is a picture of such Divine exhilaration in creation as forces us, if we are asked summarily to explain why God created the world, to affirm that He made it for fun. There is no purpose in it save the purpose of joy—the joy of the Maker in the world of His making, and the. . . . joy of the world in the world itself and in Him Who made it."[5]

Have you read Norman Habel's poem, "Lord, Did You Ever Doodle?" Here is an excerpt:

Lord,
did you ever do something silly,
just for the fun of it? . . .

Did you ever let yourself go
and take a wild ride
across the galaxies
or tie a rainbow up in knots
without a thought
of just what someone else might think
of YOU? . . .

Do you ever take the time to pause
and laugh with all of us?

Come on, God!
Join us in a wild spree across the city
with the wind blowing
sunshine in our faces.
Let's float a thousand enormous red balloons
in every court, cathedral, and park we find.
Let's set firecrackers
under every preacher and banker in town . . .

Come on, God, let's go!"[6]

When you see God as One who plays, you can let go of the foolish notion that we ought to feel guilty about our play. Many of us have formed the insidious habit of being ashamed of ourselves when we play. You hear people say: "Well, I take a vacation or a few days off, but it's only to equip myself to do a better job." I even hear people say with pride, "I never take a vacation." But when you know that God plays, you begin to see that play is our divinity in all its glory. It is salvation by grace.

And you can combine play and work. I've heard some people say that they enjoy their jobs as much as anything else they do. I know of a bank where every employee comes to work in costume on Halloween. My informant said that all the employees had a fun-filled time, but still did a solid day's work. "That's why my husband enjoys his job so much. They do things like that once or twice a month."

You wed work and play when you use a sense of humor. Jesus had a brilliant sense of humor. He said, "It is easier for a camel to go through the eye of a needle than for a rich man to inherit the kingdom of God" (Matt. 19:24). Just picture a camel in the predicament Jesus portrays! You open yourself to the kingdom of God whenever you can laugh at those frustrating people and circumstances which come in anyone's work. (Such laughter often seems impossible for me.)

Henry Ward Beecher once told his congregation that he had received a letter with only one word, "Fool." He said to his people, "I've heard of someone writing a letter and forgetting to sign his name, but this is the first time someone signed his name and forgot to write the letter."

WORK AND PLAY, THE RHYTHM OF LIFE

Work and play do not have to equal drudgery and boredom. If, in your leisure and your labor, you receive the kingdom of God like a child, you see that "work and play" is not a dichotomy. We live in one world, and the rhythm of life includes both working and playing.

The Westminster Divines said it with poetry and perception over 300 years ago. "What is the chief end of man? Man's chief end is to glorify God, and enjoy Him forever."[7] What are you waiting for?

*What does *work* mean to you? And *play*?
*Write your musings about anything that touched you in chapter 4.
*Meditate on Genesis 1:26–2:7 and Mark 10:13–16. Involve yourself in the time, place, and people of each passage. What is God's word to you, and yours to him?

QUESTIONS FOR MEDITATION OR GROUP DIALOGUE

1. What elements of your work are drudgery, and which ones are creative?
2. When do you feel play is burdensome? When does it fill you with exhilaration and joy?
3. The chapter coaxes you to a new attitude toward labor and leisure. It says: "Do your work as one laboring in the service of a God who is a mature and trusting Friend. Play like a child—spontaneously frolicking and laughing, finally falling asleep in the arms of a Father-God."
   a. How does that become more than a dream? What would it take for such a new attitude to be generated in you?
   b. Would it mean some inner surgery of the soul?
   c. Would it require more financial security—for you, for others?
   d. Would it require social change—in your corporation, union, family, and so on?
4. Some people in today's society are not totally bound to "pyramid climbing." Some will remain where they are when offered a promotion to a different city, because their current location is best for the education, spiritual growth, recreation, and safety of their entire family. Is that a way to discover God in one's work?
5. Page 48 asserts: "We need a new revolution in America—one that overturns the concept that monetary profit, whether personal or corporate, is everything." Later in this book, in the chapter on "Want and Need," the affirmative aspects of the American free enterprise system receive consideration. But for now, take some time for your group to discuss ways in which the profit motive becomes an idol for many people. What can you do to set monetary profit under God's authority—an authority of love for all life and all people?
6. Consider in depth the idea of changing the working roles for brief periods each year, i.e., a school superintendent teaches for two weeks a year, and a teacher does the work of school administration; or, a corporation president works on an assembly line for a block of time each year, and a laborer assumes the task of president. What are the advantages and the disadvantages of such an idea? At first, it may seem impractical. However, if the persons involved were to check with each other daily to be sure no crucial work is misunderstood 'or inadequately handled, the teamwork which develops could be a vibrant contact with God in your daily work. And the concept could be expanded to include other people in your place of work.
7. Can you get in touch, in your mind and feelings, with the truth that God plays? Will you let yourself be playful, accepting play as a gracious and authentically human activity? What do you do for just pure fun?

5.

Woman and Man

Ephesians 5:1, 2, 21–23

A male friend of mine, in previewing this chapter, wondered at the sequence in my title. He said: "Why *woman*, and then, man?"

When my twenty-year-old daughter saw the rough draft, she remembered the titles of the previous meditations and said: "You've written on *alone* and belonging, *work* and play, *noise* and silence, and now *woman* and man. Why did you arrange for woman to stand in line with alone, work, and noise?"

At that point, I was ready to give you ten blank pages right here and let you deal with the whole subject on your own. Then I considered what lies behind those comments.

We are all seeking a sense of significance. Each of us says: "I am important!" But when we look at the words "woman" and "man," we immediately wonder about our worth as people, because these two words have become labels with certain meanings to different people. That's what I want to look at in this chapter.

WOMAN/MAN—PERSON, FRIEND, ADVOCATE

My purpose here is to show that "woman" and "man" are not simply labels, nor are they inferior/superior categories. Rather, they are parallels for words like: person, friend, advocate. Reuel Howe suggests this when he says,

"We're the two parts of creation, male and female. We are faced with the task of uniting creation."[1]

One of the major references in the Scriptures to "woman" and "man" is found in Ephesians 5. Some of you are wondering why I chose that passage of Scripture as a launching pad for this chapter. Ordinarily, it's used by people who want to defend a rigid authoritarian role for men and a submissive role for women. If we look at the passage carefully, however, we'll see a much different message.

Consider briefly the background of Ephesians 5. Paul lived in a culture of male dominance. As Dr. Leonard Swidler emphasizes in his article, "Jesus Was a Feminist," women were not permitted to read the Scriptures in first-century Palestine, and women's prayers were meaningless; only a man could pray effectively. A woman could not testify in a court of law, because her word was not authoritative. A husband could divorce his wife, but a wife could not divorce her husband. A rabbi was thought to be undignified if he spoke to women in public. In the context of *that* milieu, Ephesians 5 is revolutionary.

Paul speaks to the whole church in verse 21: "Be subject to one another, out of reverence for Christ." He thus begins with a definition of the way we order human relationships, if we are followers of Christ. We are mutually responsible each to the other. On that basis he considers the relationship between wife and husband. He says (v. 22): "Wives, be subject to your husbands" (who, in v. 21, are already subject to their wives) "as to the Lord." That last phrase could be more properly translated: "As is fitting in the Lord" (see Col. 3:18).

Paul then says: "For the husband is the head of the wife, as Christ is head of the church." We are usually so bewildered (or irritated) by the first part of that statement that we miss the last phrase. The culture of the day assumed that the husband was the head of the wife—but the writer here is adding a wholly new dimension to the role of the husband. He is saying: "The kind of head you're meant to be is shown in the relationship Christ has with the church." Christ died for the church.

Go on to verse 24: "As the church is subject to Christ, so let wives be subject in everything to their husbands." Again, the emphasis is on the relationship between the church and Christ. What kind of subjection do we have to him? We're bound to him with the cord of gentle and unfettering love, and that's the kind of binding relationship wives and husbands are to have with each other. The entire passage proclaims that husbands and wives, women and men, are to order their lives together on the basis of the relationship which Christ and the church have with each other. That must have struck some of those first-century readers like a thunderbolt.

Notice also verses 1 and 2 of Ephesians 5, which introduce the entire thought pattern for that chapter. "Therefore, be imitators of God as beloved children, and walk in love as Christ loved us." Everything the author has to say about the male-female relationship is based on that introduction.

Dr. Dallas Roark has written a new biography of Dietrich Bonhoeffer, which contains a similar insight. He develops Bonhoeffer's thinking with respect to Genesis 2:24, 25, a part of which is quoted in Ephesians 5:31: "Therefore, a man leaves his father and mother and joins to his wife, and the two become one." Genesis adds, "The man and his wife were both naked and they were not ashamed." Now hear what Bonhoeffer says: "The profundity of this union—man and woman in the community of love, is related to the Church, which showed its original form in Adam and Eve. Where love exists, there is no shame. Where shame prevails, it is because one person cannot accept another as a gift from God."[2]

MAN/WOMAN: LANGUAGE OF HUMAN LIBERATION

Man and woman are not words meant to freeze people into molds. They are key words in the language of human liberation. This leads us to a very basic question. How do we find our identity as a man or a woman? First and foremost, we could see ourselves, to use the Ephesian phrase, as "beloved children of God." And, as his children, we could see our maleness and femaleness as ways to release the gifts of other people. One person said to me, "You'll never find any freedom for yourself unless you're seeking freedom for other persons."

Just what are the unique attributes of the male, or the female? This is a question currently under serious investigation. Of course, women have the sole capacity to bear children. And male sperm is the sole determinant of the sex of the child. Beyond these, we have great difficulty in determining other attributes which are exclusively male, or exclusively female. For a long time, many people felt that the sexual functions engender certain natural capacities in women, and other tendencies in men, viz.: women may have natural inclinations toward tenderness and nurturing; men may naturally lean toward initiative and assertiveness. In recent years, this conclusion has been decisively challenged.

Wherever you stand on that issue, let a woman make available to a man any hints she may have as he seeks to increase his own capacity to be tender and nurture growth in others. And let a man be open to sharing with a woman any insight he may possess as she develops her own being as initiator and doer. Whatever we discover in the future about our inherent beings as male or female, we can use any sexually derived gifts not to close the doors to new behavior, but as keys to unlock individual destinies.

It is so easy to let society's images of man and woman almost suffocate others, and ourselves. I remember an experience my wife and I once had with eight other couples in a week-long workshop. Part of the time we met in groups of three couples each; part of the time all nine couples met together. Two days before we left, we were all meeting in one group for a two-hour session. At the outset of that meeting, our director questioned one of the women in the group. Her husband had a terrible habit of always answering for her. On this particular occasion, after the director's first question, her husband said, "Well, she's not very articulate on that subject." The director asked her another question, and her spouse again replied, "She and I haven't discussed that as yet." The director asked her yet a third question, and the husband said, "Well, she'll have to think about that one for a while."

This went on for two or three more questions, until finally the woman burst through her frustration, beat her fist on the table, and loudly gasped, "I want to speak! I have something *I* want to say!"

You and I hope that's an extreme situation, but it happens. Our group worked with that man and woman for another two hours and their encounter became a breakthrough to new freedom and a greater love on the part of both of them.

When the descriptions "woman" and "man" stifle people and strip them of self-respect, they become destructive words. One woman said to me not long ago, "I'm not eager to abandon my role as wife and mother. I've loved that. I like to cook, I enjoy my home, I adore my children. I don't want to let go of those things. But the women I know who are really hurting are those who are told that they're not as capable or intelligent as men. Some men say to women, in that subtle nonverbal language: 'Don't forget: you're just a woman.'"

On the other hand, a man in our parish has another view. He said to me: "Sometimes I get the impression from Women's Lib that men should no longer be assertive. But I like to make decisions. I enjoy starting things in motion."

William Emerson helps our perspective by giving us an exciting insight into what is happening with today's young people. Their clothes are similar, and they take similar risks. But they're not nearly so suspicious of each other, nor are they afraid of life. "Oh, the prisons haven't been torn down yet, but the new regime is releasing prisoners by the millions."[3]

One mother told me about her married son in college, who of necessity spends some of his time cooking, keeping house, and doing the laundry. A fraternity brother dropped in while he was running the vacuum sweeper, and he wasn't even embarrassed. He decides what he does on the basis of his wife's needs as well as his own. It hasn't lessened his own initiative. He's pursuing his professional goals with more determination than ever.

We can celebrate the new opportunities daily being created for women and men in our society. Women seek equal employment opportunities with nondiscriminatory salaries. This trend is cause for rejoicing. It also deserves the church's full support, and initiative where needed. At the same time, men are blazing some new trails. Roosevelt Grier, a former professional football player, has given new credibility to needlepoint for all persons. He has shown that pursuits long considered "strictly feminine" are open to men.

And the sexual relationship becomes a greater adventure as this new openness develops. Women are free to be assertive in intimate sexuality. And men are free to be receivers as well as initiators. In the spirit of Christ's love, men and women who are brothers and sisters in Christ are free to show some affection without the fear of disapproval. In the Christian life style persons of the same sex can hug each other without embarrassment.

FREEDOM AND THREAT

Certainly this new freedom brings with it a threatening responsibility. Now we have to make a host of new decisions. But that's where Christ's gospel has always led us. He also gives us the kind of help that will make this an exciting pilgrimage rather than a debilitating experience. His gospel says we always live under the grace and sovereignty of God. "Be imitators of God as beloved children" (Eph. 5:1). Those qualities of God come to us in the body of Christ, the church. In the faith community, at least in our better moments, there are no denigrating labels.

In my former parish, in a dialogue group program, a woman said to the members of her group at the conclusion of their meetings, "I want to thank you for doing for me something that has never happened before in my life. Most of the time my husband treats me like I'm a feminine functionary. I'm afraid my children deal with me as though I were a matron. And it appears that society would like to relegate me to being a sex symbol. But you people have affirmed me as a self. And now I am beginning to find my own being."

That's what it means to say to a man or a woman, "Be subject to one another out of reverence for Christ" (Eph. 5:21).

*When you see the words *woman* and *man*, what other words come to mind?
*Work with the questions on p. 63 and write whenever your ideas flow.
*Listen with the "inner you" to Ephesians 5:1, 2, 21–33.

QUESTIONS FOR MEDITATION OR GROUP DIALOGUE

1. What does it mean to you to be a woman? A man?
2. On what basis do you develop your sexual identity?
3. What would happen, in practical terms, if you saw your maleness or femaleness as a way ". . . to release the gifts of other people"? How do you think other people would respond to you?
4. The "traditional roles" for men and women are no longer clearly fixed. There is freedom now, for variations in the ways men and women determine their roles in life. Do you consider this helpful or harmful? What does it do to you?
5. The liberating of men and women brings with it new responsibility. Our decisions about femaleness and maleness aren't so automatic as they used to be. How are you working with this new reality? Is it primarily a threat, or an opportunity?
6. What did you hear from this chapter in terms of the gospel's message to woman and man—and to you?

6.

Doubt and Faith

Colossians 1:15–20

Have you ever struggled with doubt about God? The other morning as I was shaving, the thought came crashing in on me: *What if there is no God?* It reminded me of a time in college when for two solid years the same question haunted me.

As I look back on those early doubts, I see them as a grasping for faith, expressed as resistance to a magnetism I could not turn off. But when those doubts were assailing me, they were devastating; sometimes paralyzing.

As I worked on this chapter I kept wishing that I could write an entire book on the subject. There are probably as many different positions today on the doubt/faith issue as there are people. We may start with the person who says, "I have decided that there is no God and there's no doubt about it," and go on to the one who says, "I know there is a God, but I'm not very concerned about my relationship with him." Then there is the person who proclaims, "I know God and I feel very certain of my standing with him." So we may approach this question from many different angles. Yet there is one perspective we all share. We know that doubt is inevitable, and faith is inviting. So the question is—how do we move between doubt and faith in a way that keeps integrity with both God and ourselves?

FAITH AND DOUBT: DEFENSE MECHANISMS?

First let's recognize that either doubt or faith *can* be mere mechanisms. If you have arrived at faith by a route of conformity or convenience, your faith is much more abhorrent to God than is doubt. The person who says, "I'm going to be a church member because it's an honorable and conventional way to be hatched, matched, and dispatched," has arrived at a faith which is a tool of manipulation. The person who clings to a faith that is smug and self-righteous, unwilling to be open to any change, worships only numb religion, not God. The doubter at least takes seriously the question of God.

On the other hand, doubt can be a form of bland neutrality. Doubt can be rooted in false pride and intellectual arrogance. It can be a way of using the mind as a defense against God. I may doubt because I'm afraid to commit myself to the One who will evoke demanding and even heroic changes in my self-satisfied life. One person said to me, "If the hot-wire of faith in God ever really gets plugged into a person, think of the changes he would have to make."

THE NEED FOR INTELLECTUAL HONESTY

We need to approach the doubt/faith question with intellectual honesty. The Christian gospel doesn't require a person to become an intellectual invalid before he takes the first step of faith. Neither does it say that the only way I can believe in God is to encompass him with my mind. Interestingly, this would lead me to create God in my own image, rather than the reverse.

One way to approach doubt and faith as a thinking person is to begin by being honest about one's disbelief. Atheists and agnostics are fond of raising the question: "How can you intellectually defend faith?" But if our arguments are going to have integrity, don't we have to turn that question around? How can you reasonably defend doubt? Of course, you can immediately think of several reasons for doubt. But what happens when those reasons are subjected to honest inquiry? Do the doubts hold up when they are set over against the claims of faith?

One of our problems is that we forget the basic issue. Who is the God in whom we do or do not believe? Louis

Cassels tells of one great preacher who responded to disbelief with astute perception:

> During his long career as pastor of New York's Riverside Church, the late Harry Emerson Fosdick spent many hours counseling students from nearby Columbia University. One evening a distraught young man burst into his study and announced:
>
> "I have decided that I cannot and do not believe in God."
>
> "All right," Dr. Fosdick replied. "But describe for me the God you don't believe in."
>
> The student proceeded to sketch his idea of God. When he finished, Dr. Fosdick said:
>
> "Well, we're in the same boat. I don't believe in that God either."[1]

FALSE CONCEPTIONS OF GOD

There are many false conceptions about God that aren't worthy of our belief. Let's look at some of them.

God the ogre. All he does is make us feel terrible and worthless. There is no such God.

God the old man. He sits above the clouds and looks at the world with curiosity, keeping score of good and bad deeds.

God the heavenly magician. He is found only in events that cannot be explained. This God is consigned to freakish happenings or astonishing incidents that defy logical interpretation. He is the one to whom people pray when they need to be rescued from an otherwise hopeless situation.

Or God the "overgrown clergyman in a box." He is sedate, dignified, and found only with nice people in nice places.

God is none of these.

HOW THE GOSPEL VIEWS GOD

If we're going to look honestly at doubt vis-à-vis faith, shouldn't we begin by considering the basic claim the Christian gospel makes concerning God? We find that assertion in one succinct affirmation in the letter to the Colossians: "Now Christ is the visible expression of the invisible God" (Col. 1:15a, Phillips). Look at that statement with me for a moment. Let's see the power that is in it. It doesn't tell us that Christ is an example of the perfect human being, although that may be true. It doesn't say that if we listen to his teaching, we will discover the way to live an upright life, although that also may be valid. Instead, we are given to understand that when we look at Jesus Christ, we see who God is. And when this Christ begins somehow to affect our lives, God happens to us. "Christ is the visible expression of the invisible God."

Think how revolutionary that thought is. If Christ is God's way of expressing himself, then God is not "up there." He's right here. He is not the champion of the righteous, but the Friend of sinners. He is not the "most popular person on campus," but he is "despised and rejected by men" (Isa. 53:3a). He is not an indulgent grandfather; rather he is a demanding Lord. He calls us to make all other loyalties secondary in order to follow him. And he is not a God who simply observes people for his own amusement, but he is a God who gets so involved in humanity that he cries. He expresses intense anger, and suffers loneliness, and sinks into despair, and finally dies for the sake of people who couldn't care less.

We may never be able to answer every question we have about Jesus. You may ask, "How can I believe he was born of a virgin?" Or your question may be, "When he rose from the dead, was it a physical resurrection?" Such questions are unrelenting for some people. But we can know that in Christ, God *is* our risen Companion and Leader, or to use the traditional words, our Savior and Lord.

This leads me to a response we can make to the most frequently expressed criticism of faith, or as some may want to put it, "assertion of doubt." Many people say: "I want to be my own man [or woman]. I want to be free from any kind of religious crutch, and I don't want to be lured into a somnambulistic, religious conformity." Both the atheists, who try to convince the world of their intellectual honesty, and the agnostics see a belief in God as a limitation on their humanity and self-reliance, and on their freedom and creativity. But commitment to the God we know in Christ gives us a new perspective toward all humanity. In Christ we can see every person's humanness as a special gift. In him we discover new resources of trust for developing a self that is reliable. This frees us from phony religion. And in him we can have new confidence in our own creativity.

How and Where Do We Meet God?

Yet there is still a central question. If God is the God we know in Christ, how and where do we meet him? How do we know that he's really there? Consider this illustration by John B. Cobb, Jr.:

> Suppose we are listening to stereophonic music in a dark room. Is the music an object? That is hardly a useful category. It can neither be seen nor touched, and it cannot be located as being at some one place. It "fills" the room and may simultaneously "fill" many other rooms as well. It is profoundly subjective in that it stirs our depths and permeates our whole experience. Yet it is profoundly objective in that it comes to us from without and has a pattern we do not determine. . . .
>
> The presence of God is much more like the presence of music than like that of a rock or a machine. It is like that of music in being intensely subjective. But like music it is also objective in that it comes to us from beyond our own being and determination.[2]

We don't come to the presence of God in an automatic way. But if we see that God is always pursuing *reconciliation* in human experience, then we can authentically meet him. That's part of what I think the Letter to the Colossians means when it says: ". . . Through [Christ] God planned to reconcile in his own person, as it were, everything on earth and everything in heaven by virtue of the sacrifice of the cross" (Col. 1:20, Phillips).

Have you thought of the ways in which God reconciles you to himself? Whenever you experience self-respect, whenever the realization occurs to you that you are a self worth giving to the world, you have been reconciled to God. And when you feel the raw edges of disrespect for yourself, you are searching for that reconciliation.

At those moments when we create or recover a relationship of trust with someone else, we have been reconciled to God. And when we experience the agony of being alienated from another, we are asking God for help in restoring that relationship.

Such a theology can lead us to meet God in that powerful divine/human encounter that we call prayer. It can enable us to *know* God in ways far more profound and intimate than intellectual enlightenment.

But where does doubt fit into this reconciled relationship? That's where we all need to be far more compassionate and sensitive than we have ever been. We need to remember that biblical history is the story of a people who walked between doubt and faith and back again. We need to see doubt as part of the faith journey. Your faith may well lead someone else through the morass of doubt, and his doubt may well cause you to reexamine and expand your faith. Together we can begin to see doubt, painful as it is, as part of our relationship with God. Even the person who says, "There is no God," takes the trouble to ignore him, which is still a witness to his presence. And those of us who experience detours along the way of our faith pilgrimage can view doubt as a gnawing emptiness that yearns to be filled. Even in the depth of despair or near the breaking point of bewilderment, doubt can be creative.

A member of our church related to me an experience of many years ago, when doubt almost consumed his life. He said, "My wife died, and a few weeks later my son was taken into the armed services. I felt totally abandoned. I doubted. I railed against God. I said, 'God, if you are there, how can you possibly let this happen?' Somehow, I went on living as though God were still real. Even though I couldn't think or feel faith, I acted in faith. And in time my thoughts and feelings caught up with my actions."

There are creative ways to move between doubt and faith. We can be honest and enabling companions with each other as we make that journey.

But remember our venture is not an aimless search for a compatible religious idea. If our pilgrimage is to take us homeward, it will lead us to commitment to a Person. Sooner or later we have to stop wandering around the doubt-faith circle and take a stand, even if we have not answered every question.

Why do we approach the question of God and his credibility in Jesus Christ? Not because we are looking for a spiritual good luck charm to add to our symbols of success. Not even because sophistication demands that we deal with the God-issue. Beneath the surface of our lives, there is a personal yearning and it will not subside.

We grapple with Jesus because we need him. We need a steady and ultimate friendship and he is such a friend. We need someone worthy of our total loyalty, and only he can claim our devotion without flinching when we ask: "Jesus, are you worth it?"

THE NAME IS SAVIOR

Jesus Christ is worthy of the one name that is deeper than even friend. The name is Savior. Each of us needs to be touched by him. You may recognize him by experiencing his renewing forgiveness, freeing you from the prison of self-defeat. You may come to know him by discovering as I did that commitment to him as your Savior gives authentic purpose to your life. You may finally decide to belong to him as a result of one of life's surprises or shocks.

Mind you, Christ will not solve all our doubts. The pathway of life with him greets us every morning, but it is by no means smooth and easy. We will struggle with faith issues all our lives. But Christ makes us aware that we need something else more deeply than the answers to all our doubts.

I am personally convinced that the resurrection power of Christ is the one contemporary magnet capable of attracting the many opposites in our world and in ourselves. *He* is the Reconciler—yours, mine, and the world's. In him God offers to take the inward and outward walls around your life and turn them into bridges. Then doubt, once an enemy, becomes a nagging yet challenging companion. And faith grows, one step at a time, no matter where you are in the unpredictable hills and valleys of your day-by-day living.

*How do you feel about *doubt?* And *faith?* Focus your perspective in light of my concluding questions.

*Meditate on Colossians 1:15–20. Dive into the Word. Even though the author was speaking to a people long ago, you can be one of them for a few minutes. What does God have in mind for you?

*The chapter says of Jesus: THE NAME IS SAVIOR. What does that mean to you?

QUESTIONS FOR MEDITATION OR GROUP DIALOGUE

1. Do you agree that both doubt and faith can be mere mechanisms? Is that true of your position regarding God?

2. The chapter asks: "Who is the God in whom we do or do not believe?" How do you answer?

3. "Christ is the visible expression of the invisible God." Think through what that means to you. What kind of God do you meet in Christ?

4. Does your faith limit your own humanity and self-reliance? What does your doubt do to your sense of selfhood?

5. ". . . If we see that God is always pursuing *reconciliation* in human experience, then we can authentically meet him." How does reconciliation happen to you?

6. Are you willing to ". . . see doubt as part of the faith journey"? Will you recognize that doubt, when it comes, is ". . . part of your relationship with God"?

7. How can your faith encourage someone else who is beset with doubt?

8. How can your doubt be a creative force for others?

7.

Want and Need

1 John 3:11–18; Mark 10:17–22

Al Capp, in one of his "Li'l Abner" cartoons, portrays a popular and prosperous singer riding through Dogpatch in her chauffeur-driven Cadillac. She sees an orphanage and tells the driver to pull over. She announces, "I'm going to contribute $10,000 to those needy orphans," and organizes a benefit performance. Throngs of people attend. But over in one corner sits Li'l Abe Yokum. He's bored. Head in his hands, he mutters to himself, "All I really *wanted* was a good hamburger."

What is the difference between need and want?

Want Is Desire, Want Is "More"

Want is a child who is not able to decide which toy to play with for the next thirty seconds on Christmas morning. Want is the glitter and attraction of a sparkling piece of jewelry. Though you could easily get along without it, you desire it very much. Want is *more*.

Some years ago there was a classic movie entitled *Key Largo*. It starred Humphrey Bogart and Edward G. Robinson. There's a scene in the movie in which Bogart says to Robinson, "Rocky, what you really want out of life is more." Rocky's face lights up and he says, "Yeh, dat's what I want—more!"

Our society tells us we ought to have more—all the

time. It tells us that luxury is necessity. It manipulates our wants. How many advertisements have you see which entice you to buy something quite optional to you, with the persuasion that deep down you truly need it?

You can also define "want" in religious terms. Some persons' life-affirmations sound like this: "If I devote myself to God, that will make me prosperous and all my problems will be resolved."

I'll never forget hearing one person say, "I committed my life to Christ, and, as a result, I have the scalps of seven of my competitors hanging on my belt." He boldly used religion to get the things of this world that he wanted. American civil religion bolsters such an attitude by asserting that the United States, being a "Christian" country, has more than most other countries because God is rewarding us.

NEED: THE BASICS

Need, on the other hand, is something deeper. You can define need as the requirements for being at home on this planet. Everyone has basic needs: a need for food, a need for shelter, a need for purpose in living, and a need for friendship with God and with people.

But go a step beyond that, and define *need* in terms of your need to share those basic requirements with other people, so that they and you can truly *live*. That's the radical definition Jesus gave to eternal life.

Members of the early church reflected Jesus' position. Look at these startling words in 1 John: "But if any one has the world's goods and sees his brother in need, yet closes his heart against him, how does God's love abide in him?" (3:17).

That is a probing question for us. In spite of inflation most Americans continue to live in overabundance. *Need* is a word we seldom use in speaking of ourselves. But our prosperity works against us.

For example, why has the energy crisis of recent years been so traumatic for us Americans? Certainly there is confusion over who causes the inadequate flow of available energy at a given time. And we are angry when those who have oil use their supplies to bleed our economy. But why do we have such difficulty facing inevitable shortages? Because affluence has hypnotized us into believing that we have a right to be greedy. We complain that the problem is economic uncertainty but the "bottom line" is that we have increased our appetite and called it, in self-deluding terms, a higher standard of living.

Now we must manage with less and it is difficult for many people to face reality. However, if we and our fellow citizens of earth fail to confront our moment of truth, we could awaken one day to a ravaged and helpless planet. Yes, the future appears to offer alternate energy sources. In time, we may even be able to harness the sun as a reliable dynamo for more years than any of us can envision. But such a hope is only an illusion unless we listen carefully to the word that echoes in every corner today. It is a message from God himself: your planet earth is a garden to be cultivated, not a throwaway consumer commodity.

Our so-called higher living standard is primarily a dream world. In fact, blind prosperity has turned our heads away from the reality that in many ways we have been living in a world that is impoverished.

In 1975 James Armstrong told us:

> The so-called Third World [the noncommunist, noncapitalist world] is a world of powerlessness and poverty.
>
> There are 700 million illiterates in the Third World; 100 million more than there were twenty years ago.
>
> There are 230 million jobless in that world; hundreds of millions more who do not live in a "wage economy."[1]

Larry Ward, writing in 1973, moves beyond the Third World and illuminates a global crisis:

> ... right now 12,000 people starve to death every day, even in this hour of technological research.
>
> But today's crises are as nothing compared to the threats of tomorrow. ...
>
> Take this already hungry world, where two-thirds of its people are desperately undernourished. But then watch it swell by 8,000 people in the next hour ... 190,000 in the next twenty-four hours ... 72 million in the next twelve months.
>
> But those are just figures, and our minds are too accustomed to astronomical statistics. Somehow we all too often fail to translate this truth into the flesh–and–blood reality which it is. ...
>
> I see those statistics in terms of that little girl in Laos, her pretty face now like a skeleton ... as she dies of ordinary dysentery. At last a hot bowl of rice has been placed beside her, but her little body is too weakened from long–term malnutrition. All she can do, as she lies there and dies, is take one little grain of rice at a time and transfer it to the tip of her tongue.[2]

Those human realities make me very uncomfortable. They cause me to reevaluate my own circumstances. I look at the world's needs and I have to ask myself a challenging question.

I am affluent. But now I realize that some people's lives are endangered and demeaned because I have too much. What do I do? I've been tithing and giving other gifts. But an era of scarcity forces me to confront my entire life style.

SOME ECONOMIC QUESTIONS

You may find in this chapter a different concern. You may say, "Well, what do we do with the capitalist system, if we take seriously the approach you advocate?"

It would be dishonest to raise the issue of want and need without in some way emphasizing that the motives of business are not automatically greedy. Just for a moment look at our economy from the standpoint of people's needs. Private enterprise has, in many ways, been a means of turning our desire to accumulate wealth into a way of meeting the needs of many people. A company produces a product. The product is sold to people who need, or at the very least, think they need, that product. (For the moment, let's not tackle the question of who created that felt need.) In the process of producing, marketing, and servicing the product, people are paid salaries with which they can meet their own needs. A profit is realized by the company, and that profit comes back into society in investments, research, contributions, and taxes, as well as in the money used for personal and corporate purchase. This, again, is a way of meeting the needs of the people. The entire process can be seen as a reflection of the Christian understanding that people cannot live exclusively to and for themselves.

But there's another question still to be asked, if we're to keep integrity with the Christian gospel: how do we decide what to buy and sell, produce and consume, when we look at our decision-making process in light of our comparison of *want* and *need?*

After all, your wants can easily obliterate someone else's needs. For instance, you could decide that you want a large and comfortable yacht. It's good for the economy, and it's good for you. If you can afford it, that settles the matter. On the other hand, if you look at your life style in terms of need, the fact is that you probably could have just as much fun with a less expensive item of recreational equipment. You might even decide on a canoe. And you could take the financial savings and use it to help the destitute, or make it available for a revolving loan fund that benefits low-income entrepreneurs. There is a profound difference between the way we spend our money when we evaluate it on the basis of what we want, as opposed to evaluating it in terms of our needs.

Look at the question from the standpoint of the company involved in making the yachts. The gospel challenges that company to raise some new questions. How do we decide what things to produce, and how do we manufacture and sell products, when we balance the needs of humanity over the luxury of some people's wants? That leads to some complicated questions. But is that a reason to ignore the issue?

Laborers, professionals, those in business, consumers, and theologians all need to sit down together and begin to face the challenge: how do we move from an economy based on abundance to an economy based on need, without ignoring each person's need to find purpose and meaning in life?

No Vague Generality

But you may be thinking: *It's difficult for me to identify with the far-flung needs of people throughout the world. That's all so vague to me.*

Why not use some imaginative identification? Many people have found methods of standing in the shoes—and having the stomachs—of those in frightful and hopeless need. Weekend (30-hour) "fasts" have multiplied in churches across the United States. Individual people have chosen to fast one meal or one full day each week. Families have instituted "soup night" (with no other food available) one night out of every seven. In all of these ventures the money saved is given to starvation relief efforts.

Twice during a recent year I agonized and rejoiced with a small group of people in our church in what is called the "Hunger Exercise," an experience suggested by Richard Hoehn.[3] Each time there were different people in the group. For two weeks we lived on a poverty-level income for food and drink ($8.00 per week per person). We met twice a week for mutual support, and committed ourselves to prayer for each other. We were also open to become listening ears to any member of the group for whom the hunger pangs were traumatic.

At the end of the two weeks we brought together our observations and our commitments to at least one change in life style. Nearly everyone reported a constant craving for food. Some observed a sense of inspiration from the fact that we were doing this for others (we gave the difference between the $8.00 a week and what we usually spend for food to starvation relief). They further reported that this inspiration strengthened them, while the malnourished of the world are constantly ravenous for no purpose at all—every day. Both times that we tried this two-week experiment, members of the group decided on changes in personal living patterns that would benefit those in need.

The reality of poverty isn't limited to malnutrition. There are other ways to touch the experiences of the poor. Some people have made it a point to make friends with someone who is poor, for the sake of the friendship. In the process, they have learned some of the feelings of human deprivation. Others have invited foster children to live in their homes.

You may have some different ideas—other ways to identify with the earth's empty ones. Our deepest need is to find our own way to follow Jesus into the poverty and pain of our world.

ETERNAL LIFE—A QUESTION OF NEED

The Gospel of Mark tells a story of want and need. It's a tale about a rich man. He could be one of us.

Being a man of candor and deeply concerned about spiritual matters, he confronted Jesus with the question: "Good Teacher, what must I do to inherit eternal life?" (Mark 10:17b). Jesus responded, "You know the commandments: 'Do not kill, Do not commit adultery, Do not steal, Do not bear false witness, Do not defraud, Honor your father and mother'" (10:19). The man was far from satisfied, and he said, ". . . Teacher, all these I have observed from my youth" (10:20). Mark's Gospel has perceptive insight, as it records Jesus' reply: "And Jesus looking upon him loved him, and said to him, 'You lack one thing; go, sell what you have, and give to the poor, and you will have treasure in heaven; and come, follow me'" (10:21). But the man was dismayed and ". . . he went away sorrowful; for he had great possessions" (10:22b).

We usually react to that story before we realize that Jesus said what he did to meet the rich man's need. That man was seeking eternal life. Jesus, out of his love for him, said: If you are to receive eternal life, you need to give yourself in sacrificial devotion to me.

Halford Luccock tells us that: "Jesus did not tone down his message for the sake of winning a desirable disciple ... It would be easy, and sad, to imagine how many a skillful ecclesiastic would have 'handled' this 'prospect.' We can almost hear the unspoken words behind the ingratiating smile: 'There is no use to alienate a man of his stature. He will be a great addition to our strength ... He will make a good chairman of the finance committee.' "[4]

But Jesus was interested in the rich young ruler as a person. He saw him as a man in need. What he needed was radical reorientation of the purpose of his life. He needed to change direction and move toward the only goal that would bring him eternal life.

Thomas Kelly, the great Quaker theologian, echoed Jesus' approach when he wrote, "[God] plucks the world out of our hearts, loosening the chains of attachment. And He hurls the world into our hearts, where we and He together carry it in infinitely tender love."[5]

Peggy Pond Church has a poem which shows how we all will be learning to put needs over wants:

Now the frontiers are all closed.
There is no other country we can run away to.
There is no ocean we can cross over.
At last we must turn and live with one another.

We cannot escape this day any longer
We cannot continue to choose between good and evil
(the good for ourselves, the evil for our neighbors);
We must all bear the equal burden.

At last we who have been running away must turn and face it.
There is no room for hate left in the world we must live in.
Now we must learn love. We can no longer escape it.
We can no longer escape from one another.

Love is no longer a theme for eloquence, or a way of life
for a few to choose whose hearts can decide it.
  It is the sternest necessity; the unequivocal ultimatum.
  There is no other way out; there is no country we can flee to.
  There is no man on earth who must not face this task now.[6]

*If you were to express the contrast between "want" and "need" to someone else, how would you do it? Look for illustrations in your own life.

*The Questions for Meditation or Group Dialogue illuminate a "moment of truth" for the world, and for you. How do you respond?

*The biblical background for this chapter comes from 1 John 3:11–18 and Mark 10:17–22. Let yourself become part of each passage. Feel into the words and their setting. Where do you stand with God when it comes to your wants and needs?

QUESTIONS FOR MEDITATION OR GROUP DIALOGUE

1. Do you agree that our society stimulates and manipulates us to want "more" all the time? Do you think of luxury as necessity?
2. What happens to you when you face the needs of the world, especially when you view them in human beings, like the little girl in Laos mentioned by Larry Ward? When you get in touch with the needs of others, does it help you to sense your own needs? Does it inspire you to compassionate action?
3. "How do we decide what to buy and sell, produce and consume, when we look at our decision-making process in light of our comparison of *want* and *need?*"
4. The chapter suggests that "laborers, professionals, those in business, consumers, and theologians" work together on ways to move from an abundance economy to a need economy, without missing the need for human fulfillment. What can you do about that challenge?
5. The chapter gives some examples of standing in the shoes of those in need. What is God calling you to do?
6. What is the relationship between giving to those in need and eternal life? Look at yourself in light of the story from Mark 10:17–22.

8.

Weakness and Strength

2 Corinthians 12:7–10; Ephesians 3:14–16, 20, 21;
Isaiah 40:27–31

On January 31, 1977, the Associated Press reported a disheartening story. Here are some excerpts:

"Family members and close friends planned to gather today to say goodbye to Freddie Prinze, who brought laughter to millions but could not cope with the sorrow in his personal life.

"A small funeral was scheduled for 12:30 p.m. PST for the talented young comedian who shot himself in the head Friday. He left a suicide note explaining he couldn't 'take it anymore,' said police Lt. Dan Cooke.

"Friends said Prinze, who was to be buried at Old North Church of Forest Lawn, was just too young to cope with the pressures of stardom.

"James Komack, executive producer of the 'Chico and the Man' television series that made Prinze a star, said Prinze was 'the most gifted entertainer of his time' but was uncomfortable in the real world.

"... Said one friend, who asked not to be identified: 'People don't seem to be able to understand that you can be talented, good-looking, healthy, that you could have fame and fortune and still have a problem!' "

Freddie Prinze died because in most of human society, it is forbidden to be weak. We constantly strive to appear strong, even when strength isn't really in us. We pretend that we are always adequate. Our banner reads: "Only the strong survive."

Such a superhuman demand upon ourselves leads to playacting in real life. We create acceptable images of ourselves and become skillful at projecting them to others. Some years ago there was a popular song by the Beatles entitled "Eleanor Rigby." Eleanor had a mask which remained in a jar near the door. Whenever she opened the door to leave, she automatically donned her mask.

If you veil your real self as Eleanor did, you stifle creativity. For the truth is that even our weaknesses can be a source of real power. The Christian gospel is rooted in an incredible strength that was, at first, misunderstood as weakness—Jesus' death on the cross. Weakness and strength both have a significant place in this world and in the adventuresome movement we call Christianity. But have you ever thought that weakness can become God's way of making us strong?

GOD USES WEAKNESS TO MAKE US STRONG

Paul writes of his own personal weakness in 2 Corinthians 12. He calls it his "thorn in the flesh." Scholars have debated Paul's specific meaning for centuries. Some say he had malarial fever, others, epilepsy and others, offensive eye trouble. Whatever the specific malady, Paul's thorn was chronic, like a nail constantly piercing his body.

Paul pleads with God to be set free from this biting pain. And God answers: "My grace is sufficient for you, for my power is made perfect in weakness" (2 Cor. 12:9a).

Then Paul makes an awesome response to God's answer: "I will all the more gladly boast of my weaknesses, that the power of Christ may rest upon me" (2 Cor. 12:9b). ". . . For when I am weak, then I am strong" (2 Cor. 12:10b).

Paul's lot was like that of so many people. Maybe even like yours. The healing didn't come. But Paul's task was that of courageously holding onto God's companionship while he endured his pain. He saw in that partnership a new kind of strength. He could not play the self-made man. He couldn't proudly beat the drum about his rare spiritual prowess. His weakness drove him to seek God's strength every day. From sunup to sundown he was aware that he couldn't make it without God's grace. Paul was a man who knew his need. He grew close to God by moving from weakness to strength.

There are many others who have grown strong in God's power. Some have touched God's stamina when they allowed themselves to be vulnerable. Have you ever had the experience of open sharing within a small group of other Christians? After the members feel mutual trust, you can release to the others some hurt or inadequacy or fear that had been hiding in painful inner seclusion. Somehow, the other members of the group can uncover similar needs. Your common weakness turns the group to God as one, seeking his grace and strength together.

Sometimes the weakness that shows when we are vulnerable comes in the midst of a major responsibility. I once heard a man telling an auditorium full of people the story of his own pilgrimage with Christ. He had never stood before such an audience, and his manner betrayed his fears. Four or five times during his presentation, he had to stop, gulp back the tears, and ask his listeners to wait with him. They did, in hushed inspiration. His story rang more true and was full of the strength of God, because of his obvious weakness.

Other people discover God's strength while conquering a destructive weakness they had indulged for years. In desperation, a woman whose life had been steadily eroded by alcoholism went to her pastor. Haltingly, with painful embarrassment, she told him her story. Weeks of counseling followed. The first three months were stormy, full of tribulation and distress. Then, one day she knelt in her pastor's study and made a commitment to relinquish her drinking. Her pastor took her by the hand and prayed with her. He acknowledged that only God had the power she needed. He asked God to take away her desire for alcohol. The moment that prayer was uttered, the temptation for alcohol was lifted from her. And it has never returned. That was fourteen years ago.

Today she is a vibrant disciple of the living Christ, spending much of her time working with drug addicts, alcoholics and prisoners. When the opportunity comes, she tells of the change in her own life. The power that she communicates is amazing. And she says, "The only way I can help others is to stay close to him. Without him I have no strength."

Sometimes God's strong way of touching weakness comes in the midst of healing, a variation on Paul's experience, yet full of reminders of grace nonetheless.

In the fall of 1976, I had my own most significant experience of God transforming weakness into strength. The experience began when I became conscious of unusual anxiety. It wasn't just the everyday tensions we all feel, but persistent internal turbulence. Day by day the feelings increased. There was no relief. Relentlessly I struggled to keep the lid on this inner frenzy, but the task was unbearable.

It was time for medical attention. I made arrangements for care of the congregation, and, together with my wife, drove to the hospital.

On the way, I was keenly aware that God was in the midst of this experience. I knew I would receive the prayers of my people in the First Presbyterian Church of Elkhart, Indiana. The renewed faith that had come to me in my week at Wellspring, five months earlier, reminded me that all was not hopeless. And during the fretful days that had led to this hospital trip, those daily times of silence, even though difficult to continue, had helped me remain in touch with God.

During my hospital stay, my doctor discovered a basic chemical imbalance which had been with me all my life. Throughout my adult life the imbalance in my body chemistry kept me moving at a constantly faster pace than is healthful. It created in me a tendency toward perpetual motion. Relaxation was nearly impossible.

But the diagnosis included a cure. My doctor prescribed a medication which provides the needed chemical equilibrium. I now feel like a new person. My insides are relieved of the turbulence that had plagued me. Oh, I still tense up in the face of heavy responsibilities, but it's a good, normal reaction. There is now a basic wholeness for me, which is a permanent gift. Strength has come out of weakness.

While I was away from my parish, God used that same transforming power with the church I serve. Suddenly without their Senior Pastor, staff members, lay leaders and the congregation drew on the strength of God for their unique task. In their moment of weakness, God gave them his spirit through each other, and they grew in spiritual vitality. They loved my wife and children with family affection. They gave me strength with hundreds of daily prayers, personal letters, and wishes of health that came with a new kind of companionship. They were telling me that they wanted to walk beside me. I, the pastor, was receiving strength from the people I am called to lead.

God uses weakness to make us strong. The strength we receive is always his. Whatever our weaknesses may be, they can turn us to God, that we may open ourselves to divine grace and power.

God Also Uses His Strength to Increase Ours

But there is another side to the issue of weakness and strength. God doesn't limit himself to drawing strength out of weakness. He often uses his strength to increase ours, building on the rocklike places within us. God's strength is also for our stronger moments.

A giant of modern Christian history lived with God's strength as the reservoir of his own. Donald Goddard presents a unique portrayal of Dietrich Bonhoeffer's last two years. In "... an imaginative reworking of the source materials ..."[1] Goddard retells the story of Bonhoeffer's life in prison and of his fight against an imminent appearance before a Nazi firing squad. It is an unforgettable narrative, revealing a man of amazing courage. In one of his letters from prison to Eberhard Bethge, Bonhoeffer wrote:

"I should like to speak of God ... not in weakness but in strength; and therefore not in death and guilt but in man's life and goodness ... God is beyond in the midst of our life. The church stands not at the boundaries where human powers give out, but in the middle of the village."[2]

Bonhoeffer reemphasizes the same theme in another letter to Bethge:

"... God is no stopgap; he must be recognized at the center of life, not when we are at the end of our resources; it is His will to be recognized in life, and not only when death comes; in health and vigor, and not only in suffering; in our activities, and not only in sin. The ground for this lies in the revelation of God in Jesus Christ. ..."[3]

The biblical saga overflows with stories of divine strength igniting human strength. Old Testament personalities often possess phenomenal energy, given them by Yahweh. Jesus' ability to resolutely meet the ceaseless demands of his ministry is awesome. He teaches, heals, deals with crowds and individual persons alike, prays, and holds together a faltering, bewildered band of disciples. All the while he communicates steadfastly that the presence of God has arrived, in a new and vibrant way. And Paul the apostle makes us long for his seemingly endless endurance, despite his thorn in the flesh.

The source of all this power is spiritual. We must never forget that strength is a word of the Spirit. Here is the truth that emerges in the Gospel like an unbelievable adventure story. We can live in intimate closeness with God who imparts his mighty power to us.

The writer of Ephesians knew this secret as the inner communion of his life: "I ask God from the wealth of his glory to give you power through his Spirit to be strong in your inner selves . . ." (Eph. 3:16, TEV). He deepens that affirmation when he writes: "To him who by means of his power working in us to do so much more than we can ever ask for, or even think of . . ." (Eph. 3:20, TEV).

I'm certain you know people who are inwardly strong. Somehow they draw from the depths of God's spirit. Outwardly they also reflect a deepening strength. I'm going to tell you about two such persons known to me.

One of them shows strength in his incredible staying power. He is a Chief Judge of a United States District Court in the midwest. Day after day he must make weighty legal decisions affecting the integrity of the law and the well-being of people. So many of those decisions are complex, with no easy way to make a determination on one side or the other. When he takes a stand on a question, criticisms frequently flow in, some of them hostile and even hysterical. In the midst of this enormous responsibility, he remains steady and faithful. He works with both law and people with a consistent fairness that is admired by those who know him. Although he keeps long hours, he manages to contribute significantly to his community and to the organized program of his church. And he keeps loving his family in ways that come through to them. He is letting God multiply his strength.

The other person who impresses me with her inspired resilience is my wife's mother, Elizabeth Neely. Her strength comes in determined commitment to Christ and in dauntless courage. She is a retired Presbyterian missionary who, at age 84, makes retirement look like the vigorous years of a graduate student. Her work in the United Presbyterian Mission in Cameroun, West Africa, began in partnership with her husband. When he died at age 50, Mom Neely went back to school to prepare herself to continue her husband's work. For nine years she pursued his dream in Cameroun and nurtured her six children as a single parent, while some of them were in schools thousands of miles away and others were with her in Africa. She tells stories of repelling attacks from driver ants in her home, caring for serious childhood accidents when no doctor was available, and going into the African bush all alone to teach evangelists.

But the mission Elizabeth Neely sustains in retirement is with her twenty-two grandchildren, stretched across the U. S. from Hampton, Virginia, to Redlands, California. These young people know that their grandmother cares. She flies, or takes the bus, moving around the country to see her brood several times a year. The purpose is to keep the flock together and to give that tender touch which can only come from grandmother. Several years ago she instituted a one-week reunion of the entire family. And without fail some thirty-five people make their annual trek to Madison-on-the-Lake, Ohio, to gather with the clan and to visit grandmother. The grandchildren feel and respect her inner stamina—it has a significant effect on their growth in Christ. The strength which makes such energy possible is apparent. She knows the Spirit of God as her Companion.

Remember, we grow on the Lord's strength, not our own. He builds with the powers we have. But he is the foundation.

Isaiah, in chapter 40, pictures for a captive and exiled Israel how inexhaustible is God's strength.

> Why do you say, O Jacob,
>   And speak, O Israel,
> "My way is hid from the Lord,
>   and my right is disregarded by
>   my God"?
> Have you not known? Have you not
>   heard?
> The Lord is the everlasting God,
>   the Creator of the ends of the
>   earth.
> He does not faint or grow weary,
>   his understanding is unsearchable.

> He gives power to the faint,
>   and to him who has no might he
>   increases strength.
> Even youths shall faint and be weary,
>   and young men shall fall exhausted;
> but they who wait for the Lord
>   shall renew their strength,
>   they shall mount up with wings like eagles,
> they shall run and not be weary,
>   they shall walk and not faint (Isa. 40:27–31).

Have you read Joni Eareckson's story of weakness and strength? The spiritual power of her pilgrimage with suffering and despair continues to grip me with deepening inspiration.

When Joni was seventeen, a swimming accident launched her into an incredible journey.

The water was blurred and cloudy that day. She had dived in where it was shallow, not knowing she had missed the deeper water until her head struck bottom with an electrifying shock that riddled her body like lightning. At first, she was too stunned to know what had happened. But, as her sister pulled her from the water, Joni realized that she couldn't move her arms or legs. A medical examination revealed that every part of her body, except her shoulders, upper arms, neck and head, was paralyzed. It's called quadriplegia. But for Joni it was more cataclysmic than any medical term can describe. For her, it was horror.

From the time Joni entered the hospital she endured indignities that eroded her soul. While still in the emergency room, Joni's head was shaved. As she was falling asleep from an injection of a relaxant she heard the sound of a drill biting into her skull. When she awoke later in her hospital room, she discovered a metal apparatus fastened to her skull, lifting her head away from her body. Hallucinations and nightmares from the necessary drugs haunted her. She lived in a Stryker Frame, a canvas structure made of two supports, with Joni sandwiched in between. Her only outlet was an opening for her face. The stress of that awkward existence seemed never-ending.

But more devastating than all of these was the despair that infected her spirit. Where was God in this unbelievable maze of helplessness?

She decided that God would help her to walk again. But

it didn't happen. At the urging of a fellow patient Joni sought refuge in atheistic philosophies. But they were empty. Then she relentlessly affirmed that God would at least give her the use of her hands. Again, hope became hopeless. She met a handsome Christian young man. Against her, and his, better judgment, they fell in love. She had thought marriage for her was unrealistic, but this made her believe that it was really possible for her. Until—the young man walked into her room one day and simply told her goodbye. The shock was almost unbearable.

It was at this point that Joni came to a moment of truth. She had been praying for and believing what she wanted, and what she believed God wanted. She began to see that the real heart of faith is surrender to God, just being in his hands, turning everything over to him.

And then the miracle came. Joni actually began to see her paralysis as a blessing. The strength started to flow out of weakness. Look at the way she says it:

> Friends and family members who knew how deeply Donald and I had cared for one another were amazed at my attitude. They had expected me to fall apart. And I probably would have gone to pieces if I had not allowed God to handle the situation.
>
> I really began to see suffering in a new light—not as trials to avoid, but as opportunities to "grab," because God gives so much of His love, grace, and goodness to those who do.[4]

For Joni Eareckson, strength now flows from strength. Twelve years beyond that day when the shallow waters of Chesapeake Bay changed her life, she is spending herself and her days creatively—speaking from a wheelchair to thousands of young people of her faith in Christ and her commitment to him, and drawing with a pen held between her teeth, with her art being displayed and sold all over the United States. She says that:

> For those who love God, everything—even what happened to me at age seventeen—works together for good. God has been good to me. He has ingrained the reflection of Christ into my character, developed my happiness, my patience, my purpose in life. He has given me contentment. My art is a reflection of how God can empower someone like me to rise above circumstances.[5]

Whether your life is beset with weakness or whether you are enjoying a growing strength, God's strength is being offered to you at this very moment. It is there for the asking.

*When you see "weakness," what images come to mind? How do you envision "strength"?

*As you deal with the questions that conclude this chapter, correlate them with your own feelings about strength and weakness.

*Read the Scripture for this chapter as a living drama for you. Write the communication that happens between God and you as you meditate on: 2 Corinthians 12:7–10; Ephesians 3:14–16, 20, 21; Isaiah 40:27–31.

QUESTIONS FOR MEDITATION OR GROUP DIALOGUE

1. Spend some time with the question: Can weakness "... become God's way of making us strong"?
2. In 2 Corinthians 12:9b, Paul says: "I will all the more gladly boast of my weaknesses, that the power of Christ may rest upon me." Do you sense the power of Christ resting upon you in your weaknesses?
3. In the trustful sharing of a small group of fellow Christians, you can tell the others of any pain or inadequacy that plagues you (if you want to). When several members of a group do that, it can turn the group to God in common need for his strength—and inner healing often comes. Have you known such an experience? Do you need it now?
4. Consider the statement: God can make me whole and overcome my weaknesses. Is that real for you? Do you know God as One who wants to personally help you?
5. God also uses his strength to develop ours. He is in life's vitality and stamina, as well as in weakness. Do you know God in the strength of your life? Do you meet him in your vigorous moments?
6. Are you aware that *God's own strength* is available to you? Do you tap that strength? Ponder Isaiah 40:27–31 and its power for you.

9.

Black and White

2 Corinthians 5:11–6:2

What picture do the words "black" and "white" suggest to you? When you think about "black," are your thoughts negative? Or do you recall that "black is beautiful"? Does your mental image of "white" include the concept of purity?

I asked a white person whether she thought we still place moral evaluations on the words "black" and "white." She said, "No, I think we're more semantically sophisticated today. But I'd like to hear what a black person has to say about that same question."

So I raised the issue with a black. She said, "Well, we may be more sophisticated, but I think the moral attachments are *still* there." She went to her dictionary and said, "Just look at this. The definition of black is 'dark-complexioned; Negro,' but it's also 'dirty; evil; wicked; . . . dismal; sullen'. . . . And there are the attendant words, 'blackball,' 'blacklist,' 'blacksheep,' 'blackmarket,' and so many others.[1] Look at the definition of white: 'having the color of pure snow or milk; of a light or pale color; . . . pure; innocent; . . . Caucasian.'[2] Tell me, why is black so bad?"

Those responses may be symptomatic of the current relations among racial groups. There is good news, and there is bad news. There are significant positive achievements and there are yawning chasms of injustice into which we're called to pour God's righteousness.

One example of the enigma of race relations in today's world is the way in which the concept of integration has fallen into ill repute. In the minds of many white persons, integration has become a byword for what they feel are unfair advantages for minorities. And in the thinking of a number of blacks, integration is a diluent in which racial and personal identity become a colorless amalgam.

A NEW COMMITMENT TO JUSTICE AND TRUST

We need to refresh our commitment to a world in which blacks and whites—people of every color—share life with justice, freedom and face-to-face trust. That may not happen unless we find a new way to express that commitment, one with an inherent charisma for our new era.

The 1960s and early '70s gave us a thundering call to reconciliation. Let's add to that still venturesome challenge another simple, powerful word, one for the 1980s. It's a word you probably use often, but don't think about much. The word is *respect*.

By respect, I don't mean a bland, segregated tolerance. I mean the positive regard for one another that translates into a loving black–white partnership. If there is respect among us, there will be reconciliation. The two are inseparable.

Where do we get this mutual esteem? Let's start with the Apostle Paul: "With us therefore worldly standards have ceased to count in our estimate of any man; even if once they counted in our understanding of Christ, they do so now no longer. When anyone is united to Christ, there is a new world; the old order has gone, and a new order has already begun" (2 Cor. 5:16, 17, NEB). Paul tells us that Jesus Christ has re-created the world. By joining hands with Christ you have a new way to evaluate other people, and that way is contagious. Gone are the standards of physical appearance, bank account, and social standing. No longer can you divide people into insiders versus outsiders. All the lines that become barriers between people are erased forever.

I once heard a friend put it this way: "People look at you differently when you wear an Afro. They think you've changed. And their attitude changes. A person with a new Afro walked into our office last week and the person sitting at the desk next to me said, 'Look, now he's a militant.' But he hadn't changed at all; he'd just styled his hair differently." Then she said, "To paraphrase an ancient truism, you can't judge a person by his hair."

Paul says there's only one way you can judge people: "... we are convinced that one has died for all ..." (2 Cor. 5:14a). Everyone—black or white, Afro or bald—is a person for whom Christ died.

On that foundation we can build genuine respect for blacks and whites—an admiration that will swell and overflow. But how do we do it?

CELEBRATE THE ACCOMPLISHMENTS

First let's celebrate the accomplishments that have already been made in conquering racism. A friend said to me recently: "There is still much pervasive prejudice, but let's rejoice in the advances. I am now very hopeful for the future. I once saw naked hate during the Civil Rights movement. I didn't know people could hate that much. That hatred has diminished now. We're learning that the myths of racism are not true." She said, "I'll tell you one thing that's very close to me. The white people in our neighborhood—and most of them are white—really accept me."

Another friend said, in reflecting upon his childhood, "There's such a dramatic difference between today and when I was growing up. We had one black student in my high school. He was the son of a chauffeur. They lived above a garage. He was my chemistry lab partner, and a very fine person, but we never thought about him. He was almost a nonentity. I know he was never included. I never went into a department store, a restaurant, a drugstore, or a church in my early days, where I even saw a black person, except those who were performing the most menial tasks. Now the situation has begun to change for the better."

Black culture is weaving its way into America's music and drama and style of dress. Black persons have moved into leadership positions in politics, education, commerce, television, and in the churches.

EVALUATE YOUR ATTITUDE

However, if mutual respect is to be our clarion call, we need to conduct an attitude test. Do you see yourself and others in the light of Jesus' love for every one of us? If your skin is "white," how much of your stability and meaning is based on that fact? If your skin is "black," have you capitulated your self-image to the falsehoods of racism? That's tough to avoid, since our culture taught second-class citizenship to blacks and superiority to whites for so many years.

As you test your racial outlook, you may discover some positive changes in yourself. You can build on that growth. Whatever your progress, ask yourself what you need to do to develop into a genuinely inclusive person. Ask God to lead you. He has been ready for a long time.

I believe God wants to nurture the personal feelings of blacks and whites toward each other, so that we see one another as persons instead of caricatures. Bill Pannell tells of a time when a white man wrongly ordered him and his two sons off the beach where they were swimming. He mentions the calming effect which one of his sons had on him in that incident. Then, reflecting on what it means to look ahead as he raises his two sons, he says: "The future? Exciting to be sure. We will travel, talk, ask questions, answer them. We'll fight to keep their minds clear and clean, their hearts free from those small and dirty prejudices they are sure to meet. We'll tell them about girls—about the not-so-obvious fact that girls are . . . to be loved and respected and not used. And what if the special one is not a Negro? Your daughter? Oh, I'll pour some milk on my ulcers, pick myself up from the floor, smile and passionately hope we parents have at least as much sense as our kids. . . ."[3]

When you see another person as a genuine human being, with inherent gifts and goals, achievements and needs, a deep respect for that person will seem the most natural feeling in your world.

OUR FOUNDATION: SHARED HUMANITY

An experience in my own community was built on a sense of shared humanity among whites and blacks. It may be a prophetic message, reflecting God's current goal for race relations. In the midst of a government housing program that was caught in the tangled web of bureaucracy, our church's ruling board decided to call together a coalition of black and white organizations. Our primary purpose was to give citizen leadership and support to that portion of the government program which included a redevelopment of the black ghetto, relocating families in better housing. We also set ourselves to the task of helping to meet other housing needs for citizens living in blighted areas. The name, Citizens' Coalition on Housing and Living Space, seemed to fit us best.

Few organizations have been so comprehensive in makeup. Add together a significant part of the business leadership of the community, churches black and white, the Urban League, the United Way, school-sponsored interracial parent groups, the Salvation Army, a racially mixed housing organization, a family development group, a church community service organization, and other similar groups and individuals, and you have an expansive blend of people—all with a common purpose—decent housing for the residents of a city. Each group selected representatives for the Coalition and we were on our way to action.

After a concentrated period of planning, the Coalition began its work with government officials. The results were dynamic and encouraging. Money previously frozen was thawed out for use with the ghetto housing program. Political leaders and local citizens began to see the dignity of the city and its people as their common concern. And black and white persons joined in a collaboration that revealed our basic unity. Respect grew out of working together for common goals.

JOIN AND CONQUER

Black and white people will never honor each other deeply until we do join forces, all across our land, to remove the injustices and broken relationships that still plague us. Even though our victories in conquering racism are considerable, we will achieve authentic mutual regard only when we press on and finish the task. On January 11, 1977, Vernon E. Jordan, Jr., Executive Director of the National Urban League, issued a revealing statement at the "State of Black America" Press Conference in Washington, D.C. He spoke of ". . . continued hardship for black people," and ". . . unrelenting struggle for survival in a national climate marked by recession and by majority attitudes ranging from indifference to hostility toward the plight of minorities." He also reported that ". . . employment and housing are the most crisis-ridden areas," citing not only high unemployment among black workers but an extremely serious rate of joblessness among black teenagers. Jordan observed ongoing discriminatory practices in housing, and grossly inadequate and, in some cases, detrimental efforts in housing practices. His statement preceded the Urban League's annual report, which detailed other crying needs. That was early 1977. What would be the assessment of Black America now?

QUESTIONS FOR ACTION

As you consider God's call to you in seeking a world where esteem is the word among races, do any of the following questions summon you to action?

- How can your church become an open and inclusive congregation that moves beyond society's class structure? What needs to happen so that minority people will *want* to join your congregation?
- What are you doing to help eliminate the grim futility of the ghetto?
- Should your church issue a call to interested white members of the congregation to seek membership in a black church? Or vice versa?
- When black people move into all-white neighborhoods in your city, will they be welcomed—or just tolerated? And how do you regard whites who move to black neighborhoods?
- Are you willing to take a stand for school and neighborhood integration so that there may be equal educational opportunity?

The word is respect. We use it best when we know other people as gifts of God, as companions on a common journey.

One of the great breakthroughs on the halting trek toward black-white friendship came at the beginning of 1977 with the ABC epic, *Roots*, a dramatization of Alex Haley's book. On eight consecutive nights, an estimated 50 percent of the American population watched the story of Alex Haley's family. As the drama moved from the Haley family's beginning in the Gambia, West Africa, through four generations of slavery in the United States, both black and white people were profoundly affected by the deep feelings portrayed.

Many blacks saw themselves for the first time as a people with a history—a noble, heroic history marked with incredible vitality. And those who have white skin saw themselves as linked to that history. Blacks discovered in that history a rich resource: honor, pride, a beginning for their own being. Blacks and whites were made to realize that the black man was not the creature of the white man. Kunta Kinte was his own man, with his own special origin and his own godlike destiny.

Whites winced in agony at slavery's ghastly excesses; and they were moved to humility and stirred to profound admiration toward black people. It was a monumental landmark in racial attitudes. We all saw ourselves in a kindred relationship.

We can hope that the lessons of *Roots* are still being learned today, in fresh but probably less spectacular ways. The only way for race relations to travel today is for respect to move back and forth between white and black. Then we can march together with a new, deliberate solidarity, for the justice that is wanting. It will be a different kind of marching, with our combined voices and influence, our ballots and campaigning, our worship and our Christian witness. Let us march into the mayor's office, the city council meeting, the halls of Congress, and the White House. Let's show that we believe racial healing can and will come. Let's reach for a new dream and make it reality.

*Express on paper how you react when you read "black and white."

*After you move through the Questions for Meditation or Group Dialogue write your own challenge for healing racism. Make it a challenge both for yourself and others.

*Meditate on 2 Corinthians 5:11–6:2. Rewrite in terms of the "black and white" challenge.

QUESTIONS FOR MEDITATION OR GROUP DIALOGUE

1. What is your mental image of "black"? What do you associate with "white"?

2. In race relations, the word for the '80s is *respect*. As the chapter defines it, do you feel that respect is the goal we now need to produce black-white partnership? How do *you* generate and multiply such respect?

3. In 2 Corinthians 5:14–17, Paul shows that Jesus Christ has erased all the barriers that divide people into outsiders versus insiders. Does it ring true for you to say: "Everyone—black or white, Afro or bald—is a person for whom Christ died"?

4. Do you agree that there are accomplishments to celebrate in the struggle to overcome racism? Can you celebrate some *specific* gains?

5. Try conducting the attitude test: "If your skin is 'white,' how much of your stability and meaning is based on that fact? If your skin is 'black,' have you capitulated your self-image to the falsehoods of racism?"

6. The chapter poses some "Questions for Action." Try answering some or all of those questions. Ask God to guide you in your answers.

10.
Permanence And Change

1 Corinthians 13:1–13

I'll begin this chapter by telling a story that I think is a parable of permanence and change. It's a true story.

Upon graduation from seminary I began serving three rural churches. Two of them each had twenty-five members, and the third had one hundred members. They were yoked in what is called a "larger parish." I went into that parish with a vision of reforming and recreating those churches in six months—or, if some unforeseen delays might arise—perhaps a year.

On the other hand, the members of the parish, at least many of them, held tenaciously to their traditional ways. You can imagine that we had a lot of fun. Toward the end of the year I proposed that we merge the three churches, since the three buildings were but seven miles apart, and the merger would make for a more dynamic ministry. They resisted that proposal firmly, and I pursued it with dogged determination. You might say we experienced salvation by disturbance.

I was proposing change and they were resisting it. But both the parish and I were seeking permanence in the approaches we were making. They were looking for permanence in tradition. I was looking for permanence in new steps designed to manifest the oneness of the church. They were right. And so was I. The miracle is, they endured me, and even responded to my challenge by uniting two of those churches. And I, by the grace of God, refused to become overly discouraged when they resisted. You could say that together we discovered permanence in the love of Christ—permanence that made change creative rather than destructive.

CHANGE CAN BE AN ADVENTURE

Change is sometimes exciting for all of us. We welcome it. What gives a person more pride than looking at a picture of the first moon landing? And yet, what more dramatic change can you imagine than that event? And how often do you hear people speak of their need for a change of pace?

Think of some of the renewing changes that may have happened in your life. An ugly habit conquered and laid aside. The birth of a baby. A commencement exercise. Building, and moving into, a new house. The liberating fresh air of social change that uproots injustice. A new friendship.

We say that it's a sign of maturity when a person is flexible. We even think of the word as an affirmative synonym for change. Many of today's young people, even though plagued by rootlessness, have found flexibility a means of reaching greater depth in life. For instance, I hear of many youths who graduate from college and spend two or three years traveling abroad in a Peace Corps-type life style. Then they return to school. Some adults say, "Well, they're just putting off the task of earning a living." Are we sure that it isn't, instead, a search for creative change?

Some adults welcome the renewal of change. I heard an adult say recently, "The concept of change is not as threatening or distracting to me as it was twenty years ago. Now I'm delighted to admit that I can change. Heretofore it would have been a confession of guilt. There's a new freedom for me now." Change can be an adventure.

BUT CHANGE ALSO CHALLENGES OUR STABILITY

But it can also be a threatening experience. George Bennett gives us some insight into the threat of change when he says: "Everything seems to change. We live in a flattened galaxy of one hundred billion stars that change position at the super-speed of light. An incredible number of an individual's body cells die each day. They are replaced by new cells at a slightly higher rate—until the degenerative processes of aging set in ... as you read this. ... The weather forecast will be revised. You will have less time. Everything seems to change. ...

"Change distresses us, disconcerts us, depresses us, even change for the better ... medical science lengthens life—but multiplies the problems of the elderly; our children grow 'in wisdom and stature'—and they leave us ... we mature into polished personalities—and lose the sparkle of spontaneity; knowledge increases the potential for mercy—and for mass murder.

"Change challenges our stability, and we need something stable if we are to survive."[1]

In a recent discussion I heard someone say, "When I try to find something permanent, it's very frustrating. There is nothing that is permanent, except the reality of God."

WE CRAVE PERMANENCE

But even in the face of that understanding, we continue to seek permanence here on earth. We seem to need what one person described as "something we know will always be there." There's a line in the play, *Cat on a Hot Tin Roof*, by Tennessee Williams, that resonates with our yearning for permanence. Big Daddy says: "... the human animal is a beast that dies and if he's got money he buys and buys and buys and I think the reason he buys everything he can buy is that in the back of his mind he has the crazy hope that one of his purchases will be everlasting! Which it never can be. ..."[2]

Our hunger for something everlasting is seen in the pervasive nostalgia of our day. Have you noticed how prominent nostalgia has become on television? And in contemporary music, movies, and books?

We try to find permanence in self-preservation. About ten years ago I saw a movie that portrayed what was then pure fiction, but today seems even possible. I've forgotten the title, but it was the story of an inventor who discovered an embalming fluid that would preserve a dead body in its condition on the occasion of death forever. He got an idea. He bathed himself in the fluid. Several months later he discovered that he had remained the same. He had found immortality.

"How wonderful!" you say. But was it? The movie pictured him moving through century after century, becoming steadily more miserable. At the end of five hundred years, he fell to his knees and asked to die. He begged to die. He'd found the secret of everlasting life on earth, only to realize that what he really wanted was somehow beyond himself.

We crave something deeper than an unending lease on survival. We're searching for something that is ultimately reliable—a "ground of being,"[3] to recall Paul Tillich's familiar phrase, or a "primordial reality."[4]

LOVE ALONE IS PERMANENT

There is an answer to our craving. Paul defines permanence in just three words: "Love never ends" (1 Cor. 13:8a). Paul is pointing toward the future age when Jesus returns to the world. He is showing us that when that age dawns we will realize that the future has always belonged to the love of God. Paul illustrates his meaning by telling us of some ephemeral realities that indeed cannot last: ". . . as for prophecies, they will pass away; as for tongues, they will cease; as for knowledge, it will pass away" (1 Cor. 13:8b).

Prophecy is necessary in a world still indifferent to a seeking God. But, says Paul, it is temporary. Speaking in tongues, which may be an effective expression of faith, will terminate. Knowledge, absolutely essential for the Christian called to love God with his mind, indeed is not permanent. All of that, says Paul, is transient. (We can add to his list—affluence, social prestige, and so on.) But there is one reality we will not lose—the love of God.

It may help us to take time for a brief discussion of Paul's language to better understand his meaning. He uses in this passage the Greek word *agape*, which is far more clear in Greek than our word *love* is in English.

Anders Nygren has given us a lucid description of *agape* in his book *Agape and Eros*. We can benefit from a brief summary of his thorough analysis. *Agape* is spontaneous and uncaused. It is not given because its desire is met. *Agape* is not caused by anything outside itself. God's love emanates from the nature of God. *Agape* is not based on human merit. God loves the sinner in spite of his sin, but he doesn't love the righteous person because of his righteousness. *Agape* makes fellowship with God possible. We can live with him not because we deserve to do so, or have somehow earned that privilege, but because God loves us unconditionally. And *agape* is a relentless love, hauntingly given, always seeking a response.[5]

In the First Letter of John we are told that God, by definition, is *agape* (1 John 4:8b). And, to paraphrase Paul in 1 Corinthians 13:8, when you receive or give God's *agape*, you participate in permanence. You can see God's permanent activity in the death of Jesus. Consider that event as an expression of God's unconditional love to you.

As Jesus endured the brutality of the crucifixion, it all seemed so foolish. Every bit of common sense dictated it so. You can hear the voices carping indignantly:

Jesus, you didn't have to be a martyr. If you'd made some compromises, you'd have survived the crisis and come back with your crusade another day—maybe this time to win all Jerusalem.

Besides, your disciples need you. How will they ever make it without you? They need to see your leading them. Had you yielded a point or two, your enemies would have mellowed in time. Why did you get yourself killed?

Jesus might have answered:

If only this cross were not necessary. . . . I feel as though I'm breaking in half. But it must be this way. You will never know what God's love is like if I don't face death for you. If I don't meet death and walk through it, you'll never know that forgiveness is forever.

I look at the people who live on this earth, buffeted and blown with sadness and trouble, and lost in their own indifference. And I say: they need a rock that won't break, a friend who will never forget. They need a Lord to overcome their egotism.

There is fiery pain in my body, and at moments I feel I'm all alone, abandoned. But I am hanging here to give you what you could never give yourselves—love that will hold onto you with nail-pierced hands, and never let go.

That is the permanence on which you and I can lean our loves and our world, past, present, and future.

As one person said recently, "The more confidence we have in the love of God, the less we are threatened by change." In fact, the permanence of God enacts remarkable changes. It's not static. God is far ahead of any of today's futurologists. *Agape* creates amazing, productive changes. Just look at Jesus' disciples right after the crucifixion—a disillusioned group of shattered people. But what a transformation following the resurrection and the day of Pentecost! Anyone who would listen heard from their lips the exciting, incomparable story of a living Lord who had risen from the dead. They simply overflowed with the love of the risen Christ.

LOVE CAN OUTLAST ANYTHING

J. B. Phillips's translation of Paul's Hymn to Love shows us the permanence of God in a way that is almost eternally vivid. Look at these verses: "Love ... can outlast anything. It is, in fact, the one thing that still stands when all else has fallen" (1 Cor. 13:7, 8, Phillips).

An illustration of true permanence came to me recently in a conversation I had with a friend. He and his wife had started a new program one evening a week at a community agency. "We've brought in 160 boys who are from what we might politely call 'disadvantaged' homes. We provide recreation and counseling, pay for the space, and we've recruited some people to help us. And the fun and the joy and the sense of being cared about that those boys exhibit is a sight to behold. You know, some nights I go home and I cry about those boys. Because I'd like to do so much more. If I didn't have to work for a living, I'd quit my job today and do that full time for nothing."

I asked him, "What kind of help do you need?" He replied, "I need people, more people, to work with them. And people who, having worked with those boys, will not be afraid to walk down the street alongside influential friends and go up to one of the boys and hug him." Then he said something that reached me with power: "The day I can't do that is the day I want to die."

He finished with a brief story: "A ten-year-old stole one of our basketballs. I sat down with him and I said, 'Why did you do that? Why didn't you tell me that you wanted a basketball so badly so we could have found a way to get one? Now I'll have to watch you very carefully, and we'll have to talk about that basketball some time later.' Two days later I got a letter from that boy. There were three words: 'I love you.' And he signed his name." My friend concluded, "Man, that's what it's all about. That's where I really live."

That is permanence. When you know that kind of permanence, you can cope with change, and make friends with it.

*In your own life how do you see "permanence" and "change"?
*After you work with the final questions, try writing your own philosophy for dealing with change, and with permanence.
*You can meditate on 1 Corinthians 13:1–13 for quite a while. Rewrite it in your own words, especially the words: "Love never ends" (13:8a).

QUESTIONS FOR MEDITATION OR GROUP DIALOGUE

1. Change is often adventuresome. What are some changes that have been exciting to you? What changes would you like to see happen?
2. But change is also a threat. Can you think of changes that threaten you?
3. We yearn for something stable and permanent. How do you manifest that yearning in your life?
4. In 1 Corinthians 13:8 Paul says that there is one reality that is permanent: the love of God. Can you sense the unending quality of God's love for you; for the world? Can you know the eternal nature of love as you look at Jesus on the cross and in the resurrection?
5. What does the permanence of love tell you about the priorities by which you live?
6. Can you think of times when God's love made creative changes in your life?

Footnotes

Introduction

1. For more guidance on the kind of devotional life taught by The Church of the Saviour, and for additional information on their inspiring ministry and mission, the following books by Elizabeth O'Connor are recommended:
    Our Many Selves (New York: Harper & Row, Publishers, 1971)
    Eighth Day of Creation (New York: Harper & Row, Publishers, 1963)
    Search for Silence (Waco, TX: Word Books, Publisher, 1972)
    Journey Inward, Journey Outward (New York: Harper & Row, Publishers, 1968).
    Also recommended: Gordon Cosby, *Handbook for Mission Groups* (Waco, TX: Word Books, Publisher, 1975).

Chapter 2

1. Thomas R. Kelley, *A Testament of Devotion*, with a biographical memoir by Douglas V. Steere (New York: 1941), p. 116. Harper & Row, Publishers.

Chapter 3

1. David Belgum, *Alone, Alone, All, All Alone* (St. Louis and London: Concordia Publishing House, 1972), p. 14.
2. *The Autobiography of J. Middleton Murry*, quoted in Robert E. Luccock, *The Power of His Name* (New York: Harper & Brothers, Publishers, 1960), p. 18.

Chapter 4

1. Quote from *The Boston Globe*, reprinted in Gerald Kennedy, comp., *A Second Reader's Notebook* (New York: Harper & Brothers, 1959), p. 346.
2. William Stringfellow, *Instead of Death* (New York: The Seabury Press, 1963), p. 43.

3. Max Lerner, "The Shame of the Professions," *Saturday Review,* 1 November 1975, p. 10.

4. Roger L. Shinn, *Tangled World* (New York: Charles Scribner's Sons, 1965), p. 58.

5. Alexander Miller, *The Renewal of Man;* reprinted in Kennedy, *A Second Reader's Notebook,* p. 197.

6. Excerpts from "Did You Ever Doodle?" from Norman C. Habel, *Interrobang* (Philadelphia: Fortress Press, 1969), pp. 52–53. Copyright © 1969 by Fortress Press and reprinted with the permission of the publisher.

7. "The Shorter Catechism," *The Constitution of the United Presbyterian Church in the United States of America,* part I, *Book of Confessions* (Philadelphia: The Office of the General Assembly of The United Presbyterian Church in the United States of America, 1967), 7.001.

Chapter 5

1. Reuel L. Howe, *Survival Plus* (New York: The Seabury Press, 1971), p. 124.

2. Dallas M. Roark, *Dietrich Bonhoeffer,* Makers of the Modern Theological Mind Series, ed. Bob E. Patterson (Waco, TX: Word Books, Publisher, 1972), pp. 53–54.

3. William A. Emerson, Jr., *Sin and the New American Conscience* (New York: Harper & Row, Publishers, 1974), p. 86.

Chapter 6

1. Louis Cassels, *The Reality of God* (Scottsdale, PA: Herald Press, 1972), p. 21.

2. John B. Cobb, Jr., quoted in Louis Cassels, ibid., p. 25.

Chapter 7

1. James Armstrong, *The Nation Yet to Be: Christian Mission and the New Patriotism* (New York: Friendship Press, 1975), p. 91.

2. Larry Ward, *. . . And There Will Be Famines* (Glendale, CA: G/L Regal Books, A Division of G/L Publications, 1973), pp. 4–5.

3. Richard A. Hoehn, "A Hunger Exercise," *The Christian Century,* 22 January 1975, pp. 60–63.

4. Halford Luccock in *The Interpreter's Bible,* ed. George A. Buttrick (New York: Abingdon-Cokesbury Press, 1951), 7:804.

5. Thomas R. Kelly, *A Testament of Devotion,* p. 47.

6. Peggy Pond Church, "Ultimatum," reprinted in Gerald Kennedy, comp., *A Reader's Notebook* (New York: Harper & Brothers, 1953), pp. 166–167. Used by permission.

Chapter 8

1. Donald Goddard, *The Last Days of Dietrich Bonhoeffer* (New York: Harper & Row Publishers, 1976), from the book jacket.

2. Ibid., p. 166, quoting Dietrich Bonhoeffer, *Letters and Papers from Prison.*

3. Ibid., p. 172, quoting Bonhoeffer, *Letters and Papers from Prison.*

4. Joni Eareckson with Joe Musser, *Joni* (Grand Rapids, MI: Zondervan Corp., 1976), p. 169.

5. Ibid., p. 181.

Chapter 9

1. *Webster's New World Dictionary*, ed. David Guralnik, 1968, p. 57.
2. Ibid., p. 620.
3. William E. Pannell, *My Friend, the Enemy* (Waco, TX: Word Books, 1968), p. 100.

Chapter 10

1. George F. Bennett, "The Challenge of Change," *Presbyterian Life*, 1 June 1966. Used by permission.
2. Tennessee Williams, *Cat on a Hot Tin Roof*, act II, pp. 86–87. Copyright © 1954, 1955, 1971, 1975 by Tennessee Williams. Reprinted by permission of New Directions Publishing Corporation.
3. D. Mackenzie Brown, *Ultimate Concern: Tillich in Dialogue* (New York: Harper & Row, Publishers, 1965), p. 43.
4. Randolph Crump Miller, "Empiricism and Process Theology: God Is What God Does," *The Christian Century*, 24 March 1976, p. 286.
5. A summary based on Anders Nygren, *Agape and Eros*, trans. Philip S. Watson (Philadelphia: The Westminster Press, 1953).

Social Studies Alive!®
America's Past

Chief Executive Officer: Bert Bower

Chief Operating Officer: Amy Larson

Director of Product Development: Liz Russell

Managing Editor: Laura Alavosus

Editorial Project Manager: Lara Fox

Project Editor: Pat Sills

Editorial Associates: Anna Embree and Sarah Sudano

Production Manager: Lynn Sanchez

Design Manager: Jeff Kelly

Photo Edit Manager: Margee Robinson

Photo Editor: Diane Austin

Art Editor: Sarah Wildfang

Audio Manager: Katy Haun

TCi™ Teachers' Curriculum Institute
P.O. Box 50996
Palo Alto, CA 94303

Customer Service: 800-497-6138
www.teachtci.com

ISBN 978-58371-880-3

1 2 3 4 5 6 7 8 9 10 -EB- 14 13 12 11 10 09

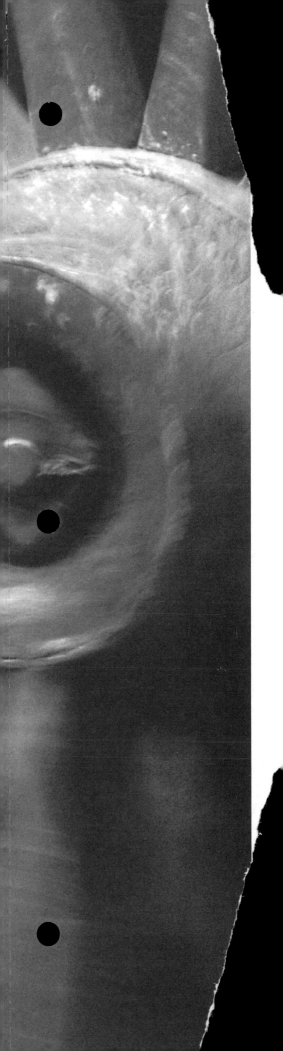

Teacher and Content Consultants

Lynn Casey, Teacher, Husmann Elementary School, Crystal Lake, Illinois

Ann Dawson, Educational Consultant, Intermediate Curriculum Specialist, Gahanna, Ohio

Nancy Einstein, Teacher, Cynwyd Elementary School, Bala Cynwyd, Pennsylvania

Leslie Frizzell, Teacher, Oakland Elementary, Bloomington, Illinois

Cathy Bonneville Hix, Teacher, Swanson Middle School, Arlington, Virginia

Shirley Jacobs, Library Media Specialist, Irving Elementary School, Bloomington, Illinois

Eleanor C. Jones, Teacher, Otice Parker Intermediate, Houston, Texas

Joan Kinder, Teacher, Ortona Elementary, Daytona Beach, Florida

Sharon Ratto, Teacher, Colonial Heights Elementary, Stockton, California

Becky Suthers, Retired Teacher, Stephen F. Austin Elementary, Weatherford, Texas

Literature Consultant

Regina M. Rees, Ph.D., Assistant Professor, Beeghly College of Education, Youngstown State University, Youngstown, Ohio

Maps

Mapping Specialists, Ltd. Madison, Wisconsin

...ies Specialist, Assessment
...California

...ing and TESOL
...condary Education,
...ncisco State
...lifornia

Contents

Geography Challenge Questions for Key Parts of the World Map

1. Label the largest continent.

1A

6. Label the ocean that touches the shores of both Europe and South America.

1A

2. Label the smallest continent.

1A

7. Label the two continents that the equator runs through.

1A

3. Locate the United States. Within its borders, label the two hemispheres in which it is located.

1A

8. Label the ocean that lies north of Europe.

1A

4. Locate Africa. Within its borders, label the hemispheres in which it is located.

1A

9. Label the ocean that touches the shores of both Asia and South America.

1A

5. Label the continent directly north of Africa.

1A

10. Label the ocean that lies to the south of Asia.

1A

Geography Challenge Questions
for Latitude and Longitude

1. Write the name of the parallel at 0° latitude.

   1B

2. Write the name of the meridian at 0° longitude.

   1B

3. Label the ocean where 15° south latitude and 90° east longitude is located.

   1B

4. Label the ocean where 45° north latitude and 45° west longitude is located.

   1B

5. Label the three continents through which 45° north latitude runs.

   1B

6. Label the ocean that lies at 75° north latitude.

   1B

7. Label the continent where 15° south latitude and 60° west longitude is located.

   1B

8. Label the continent where 30° south latitude and 135° east longitude is located.

   1B

9. Label the continent where 15° north latitude and 15° east longitude is located.

   1B

10. Label the ocean where 45° north latitude and 165° west longitude is located.

    1B

Geography Challenge Questions for Geographic Terms

1. Write the name given to a large area of sea or ocean that is partially enclosed and is larger than a bay.

   `1C`

2. Write the name given to a large body of salt water that is smaller than an ocean.

   `1C`

3. Write the name given to a body of fresh water that is completely surrounded by land.

   `1C`

4. Write the name given to a river or stream that flows into a main river.

   `1C`

5. Write the name given to a row of connected mountains.

   `1C`

6. Write the name given to a body of water that is similar to a gulf but usually smaller in size.

   `1C`

7. Write the name given to a piece of land that juts out into the water and is usually smaller or narrower than a peninsula.

   `1C`

8. Write the name given to a body of land that is surrounded by water.

   `1C`

9. Write the name given to a portion of land that is nearly surrounded by water and is connected with a larger body of land.

   `1C`

10. Write the name given to an area of land that is mostly flat and has few trees.

    `1C`

11. Write the name of the place where a river begins.

    `1C`

12. Write the name of the place where a river empties into a larger body of water.

    `1C`

13. Write the name given to a low area between ranges of mountains or hills.

    `1C`

14. Write the name given to soil deposited at the mouth of a river.

    `1C`

Directions for the *Challenge Game*

What is the latitude of Columbus, Ohio? Answer: 40 degrees north latitude	What is the main river between the Great Lakes and the Appalachian Mountains? Answer: Ohio River	What state is a peninsula surrounded by fresh water? Answer: Michigan
What river is north of Austin, Texas? Answer: Brazos River	What large lake is west of Ogden, Utah? Answer: Great Salt Lake	What state has the longest Atlantic Ocean coastline? Answer: Florida
What city on the map is closest to 35 degrees north latitude, 110 degrees west longitude? Answer: Gallup, New Mexico	What is the main mountain range in the eastern United States? Answer: Appalachian Mountains	What state capital lies between two large lakes? Answer: Lansing, Michigan
GENERAL GEOGRAPHY SKILLS	**GEOGRAPHIC FEATURES**	**STATES AND CAPITALS**

Chapter 1 Assessment

Big Ideas

Fill in the circle next to the best answer.

1. Which of these is a cardinal direction on a compass?
   ○ A. down
   ○ B. west
   ○ C. pole
   ○ D. northeast

2. Almost three-fourths of Earth's surface is covered by
   ○ A. mountains.
   ○ B. plains.
   ○ C. rainforest.
   ○ D. water.

3. What is located at 0° latitude?
   ○ A. the equator
   ○ B. the North Pole
   ○ C. the prime meridian
   ○ D. the South Pole

4. What do meridians of longitude show?
   ○ A. how close to an ocean a place is
   ○ B. how far north or south a place is
   ○ C. how far east or west a place is
   ○ D. how high above sea level a place is

5. Where does a delta form?
   ○ A. in a river valley
   ○ B. at the mouth of a river
   ○ C. at the source of a river
   ○ D. in the hills above a river

6. Which country is larger in land than the United States?
   ○ A. Brazil
   ○ B. Mexico
   ○ C. Japan
   ○ D. Canada

7. What is the most important way that rivers and lakes helped the United States to become a wealthy country?
   ○ A. They provided an environment for many kinds of fish.
   ○ B. They made it easy for people to have fun swimming.
   ○ C. They provided routes for ships and power for industry.
   ○ D. They offered beautiful scenery for travelers to admire.

Social Studies Skills

Use the map and your knowledge of social studies to complete the sentences.
Write your answers on the lines provided.

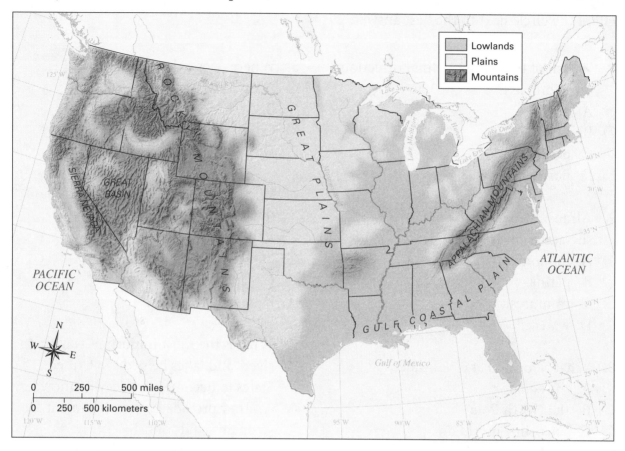

8. Two rivers that form parts of the United States border are the _____
   and the _____.

9. A tributary flowing into the Mississippi from the east is the _____.

10. A physical feature at 25°N, 90°W is the _____.

11. A land feature of the United States southeast of the Appalachian Mountains is the
    _____.

12. The western tip of Lake Ontario is located at about _____ degrees north latitude and
    _____ degrees west longitude.

Reading Further

13. You have read about Luzena Stanley Wilson and her family. Using her story and the U.S. map on the preceding page, name two major landforms the Wilsons had to cross on their trip from Missouri to the California gold rush.

_____ and _____.

14. How did rivers bring both danger and safety to the Wilsons on their journey?

Danger: _____

Safety: _____

Show You Know

15. Create a landscape that you would like to visit. Draw and label its physical features. Use the geographic terms you have learned. Use at least eight of the following terms:

bay	gulf	mountain range	sea
cape	island	peninsula	valley
delta	lake	plain	

Sioux Winter Count, 1798–1902

1818 Camp in Blackfoot Bottoms. No snow; called sand-blowing year

1819 At Good Creek. A man by the name of Joseph built traders' store.

1820 Dreams of the moon year. Next day had a sun dance.

1821 Rock Creek. Time comet fell on ground with loud noise.

1822 Dog Ghost quarrels with wife and goes away and freezes to death.

1823 Rees driven from camp, and Sioux and white men feast on corn from their fields and things left. Year of corn feast.

1824 Yellow Ree, a medicine man, painted buffalo horn white to make it snow so that they could hunt buffalo. It snowed.

1825 Year that ice broke causing flood and nearly half of camp drowned.

Chapter 2 Assessment

Big Ideas

Fill in the circle next to the best answer.

1. A natural environment includes
   - ○ A. plants.
   - ○ B. factories.
   - ○ C. stories.
   - ○ D. culture.

2. Many American Indian groups tell origin stories to
   - ○ A. teach their children the arts of warfare.
   - ○ B. explain how Earth and its people came to be.
   - ○ C. predict how the world will end.
   - ○ D. take the place of their native language.

3. According to the Hopis, where did people live at first?
   - ○ A. in the sky
   - ○ B. inside Earth
   - ○ C. across the sea
   - ○ D. in a dense forest

4. As they migrated, the first Americans went in search of big game such as
   - ○ A. whales.
   - ○ B. walruses.
   - ○ C. bears.
   - ○ D. caribou.

5. As they migrated, early American Indians had to adapt by
   - ○ A. using what was around them in nature.
   - ○ B. carrying all of their food with them.
   - ○ C. leaving old tools behind.
   - ○ D. appointing new chiefs to lead them.

6. Most early American Indians settled in places that had
   - ○ A. scarce resources.
   - ○ B. lots of rain and snow.
   - ○ C. rich natural resources.
   - ○ D. huge sheets of ice.

7. Which of these were the Inuits *least* likely to make in their environment?
   - ○ A. snow goggles made from bone
   - ○ B. an igloo built out of ice and snow
   - ○ C. a winter count on buffalo hide
   - ○ D. a float constructed from sealskin

Reading Further

8. Which natural resource did the Sioux use to record their history?
   - ○ A. tall grass for baskets
   - ○ B. eagle feather for a pen
   - ○ C. horses' hooves for ink
   - ○ D. buffalo hide for pictographs

Social Studies Skills

Use the map to answer the questions. Write your answers on the lines provided.

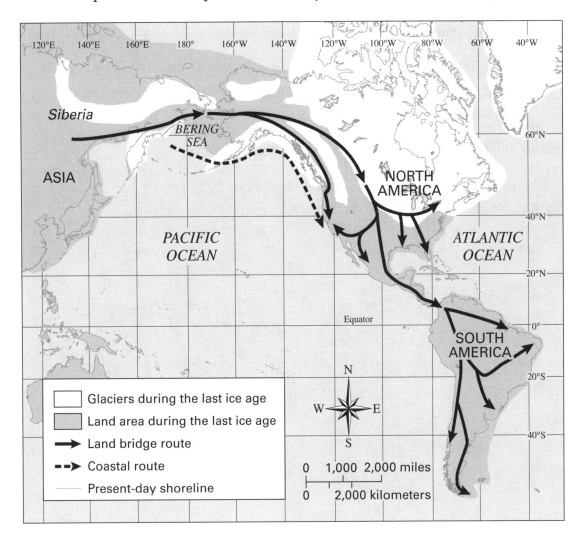

9. Most scientists believe that the first Americans came from the continent

    of _____.

10. The first Americans began their migration at a place located at about

    _____ latitude.

11. What two continents did these early people migrate to and settle in?

    _____ and _____

Show You Know

12. Look at the image your teacher projects. Draw a simple sketch of each of the three family members. Complete a large speech bubble for each person. The speech bubbles should follow these guidelines:

- One family member will tell about the migration route his or her ancestors took to reach the area where the family lives today.

- One family member will describe the environment in which the family lives and mention at least three of the natural resources.

- One family member will describe two objects the family has made and explain how these objects help them to survive in their environment.

Historical Artifacts: Homes

palm-leaf chickee
built on platform

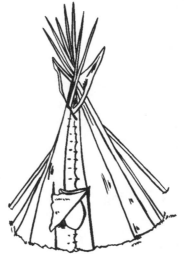

buffalo-hide tepee

birch-bark summer
wigwam

cone-shaped redwood
house

underground winter home

adobe pueblo apartments

wood house with cedar
totem poles

American Indian Cultural Regions **15**

Historical Artifacts: Clothing

waterproof cedar-bark clothing

woven cotton clothing

turkey-feather cape

woven-grass basket hat

clamshell beads on
cord necklace

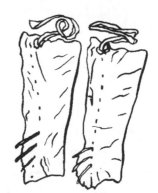

deer-hide leggings

buffalo-hide blanket

Historical Artifacts: Miscellaneous

grass basket with shells,
beads, and feathers

clay pot for storing food

digging stick with animal horn

buffalo-hide shield

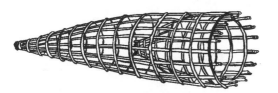

cedar and willow fish trap

cedar and birch-bark canoe

flat-bottom dugout canoe

Characteristics of Cultural Regions and Groups

Work with the members of your group to fill in your row of this chart.
Review your Reading Notes and book to find the information you need.

	Physical features	Climate	Natural resources
Southeast			
Eastern Woodlands			
Great Plains			
Plateau			
Southwest			
Californian Intermountain			
Northwest Coast			

	Northwest Coast	Californian Intermountain	Southwest	Plateau	Great Plains	Eastern Woodlands	Southeast
Housing							
Clothing							
Arts and crafts							

Show You Know

14. Because resources differed by region, many American Indian groups engaged in long-distance trade. Select two cultural regions that might have had trade relations.

Write their names on the lines: _____ and

_____

Write and illustrate a dialogue or short story about a trade encounter between American Indians from the two regions. Be sure your story or dialogue includes the following:

- one or more items available for trade from each of the two regions

- a reason why a trader from one region needs or wants to acquire an item from the other region

- drawings of at least two of the trade goods involved in the exchange

Chapter 4 Assessment

Big Ideas
Fill in the circle next to the best answer.

1. The Age of Exploration began with a search for new trade routes to
    ○ A. Africa.   ○ C. Asia.
    ○ B. America.   ○ D. Europe.

2. To study the past, an archaeologist specializes in learning from
    ○ A. artifacts.   ○ C. interviews.
    ○ B. books.   ○ D. videos.

3. "New World" was a name given to the Americas by
    ○ A. spice traders.
    ○ B. shipbuilders.
    ○ C. American Indians.
    ○ D. European explorers.

4. Sailors used astrolabes to tell
    ○ A. direction. ○ C. speed.
    ○ B. latitude.   ○ D. time.

5. A compass works by Earth's
    ○ A. large oceans.
    ○ B. magnetic field.
    ○ C. spinning on its axis.
    ○ D. orbit around the sun.

6. Why did explorers plant flags?
    ○ A. to teach Christianity
    ○ B. to help American Indians
    ○ C. to find their way back again
    ○ D. to claim land for their country

7. What religious goal inspired many European explorers?
    ○ A. to visit holy sites
    ○ B. to live in poverty
    ○ C. to spread their beliefs
    ○ D. to learn about other faiths

8. Which foods came from America?
    ○ A. wheat and rice
    ○ B. apples and pears
    ○ C. lettuce and cabbage
    ○ D. potatoes and squash

9. What do farmers do with a cash crop?
    ○ A. sell it for money
    ○ B. feed it to animals
    ○ C. eat it as soon as possible
    ○ D. freeze it to store for winter

Reading Further
10. Where in Europe did Muslims build a great center of culture and learning?
    ○ A. England
    ○ B. France
    ○ C. Italy
    ○ D. Spain

11. After Martin Luther, Europe had many wars between
    ○ A. Jews and Muslims.
    ○ B. traders and farmers.
    ○ C. sailors and explorers.
    ○ D. Protestants and Catholics.

Social Studies Skills

12. Classify the objects pictured below. Decide whether each object was either brought to the Americas from Europe or found in the Americas. Write the letter of each object in the correct part of the chart below.

A. Potatoes

B. Tobacco plant

C. Bible

D. Gold coin

E. Flag

F. Map

G. Compass

H. Astrolabe

Brought to the Americas from Europe	Found in the Americas

Show You Know

13. Select three objects you analyzed in this chapter. In the space below, follow these steps:

- Draw a simple sketch of each object.

- Label each drawing.

- Near each drawing, write one sentence explaining the use or purpose of the object.

- Write another sentence telling how the object influenced European exploration of the Americas.

Matrix Headings

Christopher Columbus

John Cabot

Juan Ponce de León

Hernán Cortés

Jacques Cartier

Francisco Vásquez de Coronado

Henry Hudson

Robert de La Salle

Personal Background

Sponsor

Motives

Dates

Route of Exploration

Impact

Illustrated Facts About European Explorers

Explorer's Name _____

Personal Background

Circle and color the figure below that represents the occupation of your explorer.

nobleman   sailor   soldier   merchant

- -

Sponsor

On the map of Europe, shade in the country that sponsored your explorer.

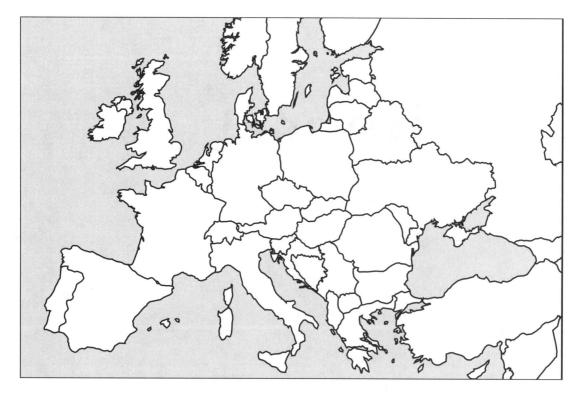

Motives

Circle and color the drawing(s) that represents your explorer's motive(s) for exploring the Americas.

to spread Christianity   to find a route to Asia   to find riches

Dates

Shade the timeline below to show the years during which your explorer explored the New World.

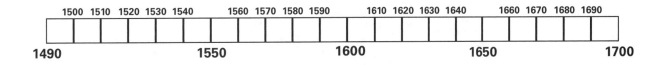

Route of Exploration

Use the map in your book to locate the route of your explorer in the New World. Draw the route on the map of North America shown at right.

Impact

Circle and color the drawings that represent ways in which your explorer affected history.

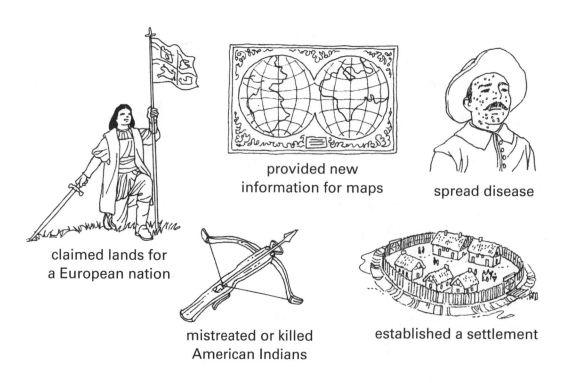

claimed lands for
a European nation

provided new
information for maps

spread disease

mistreated or killed
American Indians

established a settlement

Chapter 5 Assessment

Big Ideas
Fill in the circle next to the best answer.

1. Explorers hoped to find a Northwest Passage that would lead them
   - ○ A. across the ice of the North Pole.
   - ○ B. down the entire length of the Mississippi River.
   - ○ C. through North America to Asia.
   - ○ D. into the interior where they could find gold.

2. Why did many American Indians die from contagious diseases?
   - ○ A. They were forced to work as slaves in the mines.
   - ○ B. They got tired of giving European settlers free food.
   - ○ C. They did not have the technology of gunpowder or swords.
   - ○ D. They were exposed for the first time to some kinds of sicknesses.

3. Why did the rulers of Spain want a shorter route to the East Indies?
   - ○ A. to practice fighting wars
   - ○ B. to study a different culture
   - ○ C. to send away their prisoners
   - ○ D. to get silks and spices

4. How is a colony different from other places in which people settle?
   - ○ A. It is ruled by another country.
   - ○ B. It was started many years ago.
   - ○ C. It is designed to be temporary.
   - ○ D. It has a very simple way of life.

5. Juan Ponce de León looked for
   - ○ A. the Seven Cities of Gold.
   - ○ B. a shortcut to Asia.
   - ○ C. a site for a mission.
   - ○ D. the fountain of youth.

6. Hernán Cortés fought against
   - ○ A. the Aztecs in Mexico.
   - ○ B. the Seminoles in Florida.
   - ○ C. the Incas in South America.
   - ○ D. the Mayas in Central America.

7. Which man explored what is now the southwestern United States?
   - ○ A. Cartier
   - ○ B. Coronado
   - ○ C. Cabot
   - ○ D. Hudson

8. Which river did La Salle explore?
   - ○ A. Colorado
   - ○ B. Hudson
   - ○ C. Mississippi
   - ○ D. Rio Grande

Reading Further

9. What was the first permanent European settlement in the United States?
   - ○ A. Fort Caroline
   - ○ B. Cibola
   - ○ C. St. Augustine
   - ○ D. San Salvador

10. Why did the Spanish attack Fort Caroline?
    - ○ A. They were hoping that it would help them conquer Mexico.
    - ○ B. They did not want the French to challenge their rule in America.
    - ○ C. They wanted revenge for American Indian attacks on their fort.
    - ○ D. They hoped to discover a new route to the Pacific Ocean.

Social Studies Skills

Use the timeline and your knowledge of social studies to answer the questions. Write your answers on the lines provided.

Date of First or Most Famous Expedition

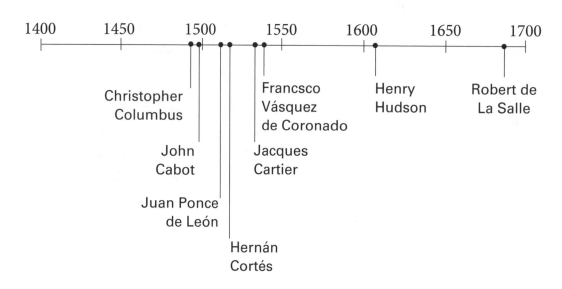

11. Give the beginning and ending dates of the century in which the most expeditions took place _____.

12. Who is the last conquistador shown on the timeline? _____

13. Which men explored before 1500?
    _____ and _____

14. Whose expedition took place soon after Jacques Cartier's voyage?

    _____

Show You Know

15. In the space below or on a separate piece of paper, design a monument to European explorers. The monument should include the following:

- human figures or visual symbols that represent the positive and negative impacts of the explorers

- a plaque that explains the monument and describes the positive and negative impacts of the explorers

Directions for Act-It-Outs

You will work in a small group to bring to life images of three settlements: Roanoke, Jamestown, and Plymouth. Your teacher will select one member from your group to play the part of your assigned figure. A reporter will interview figures that appear in the three images. Follow the directions in each section to create your act-it-out.

Roanoke

To prepare for the Roanoke act-it-out, follow these steps:

Step 1: After you have read Section 6.2 of your book, discuss the questions below and make sure everyone can answer each one.

- Why did people move to Roanoke?
- What hardships did these settlers face?
- How did the American Indians in the area treat these first settlers?
- What do you think happened to the people who settled here?
- Why do you think the settlement failed?
- What do you think the people could have done to make the settlement successful?

Step 2: Discuss how the person who is chosen to perform can make the character come alive. Use visual and written information to make your presentation of the character realistic. Collect simple props that you can use during the act-it-out.

Jamestown

To prepare for the Jamestown act-it-out, follow these steps:

Step 1: After you have read Section 6.3 of your book, discuss the questions below and make sure everyone can answer each question.

- Why did you come to Jamestown?
- What hardships did you face when you first arrived?
- What mistakes did you make in the beginning that made survival even more difficult?
- How did the American Indians in the area treat you when you first arrived?
- What do you think of your leader, Captain John Smith?
- How did life improve for you after 1607?
- Why do you think your settlement has been successful?

Step 2: Discuss how the person who is chosen to perform can make the character come alive. Use visual and written information to make your presentation of the character realistic. Collect simple props that you can use during the act-it-out.

Social Studies Skills

Use the picture below of the Pilgrims in Plymouth and your knowledge of Social Studies to answer the questions.

11. What time of year is shown in this picture? _____

12. What are the settlers building? _____

13. What natural resource are the settlers using? How are they using it?

    _____

    _____

14. Looking at this scene, name three tools that the settlers probably brought with them from England.

    _____

    _____

Show You Know

15. Suppose that you are one of the colonists at Jamestown. A ship will soon leave for England, and the captain has offered to carry letters from the colonists. Write a letter to a friend or relative who still lives in England. Your letter should follow the correct format for a friendly letter and should include these elements:

- Explanation of why you came to Jamestown.

- Description of the colony and its surroundings.

- Hardships or challenges the colonists have faced.

- Ways in which the colony has overcome the hardships or challenges.

- Advice to help your friend or relative decide whether to move to Jamestown. You may recommend coming and give reasons; recommend staying in England and give reasons; leave the decision open or list factors on both sides that your friend or relative should consider in making the decision.

Steps for Preparing a Colonial Billboard

Work with your group to create a billboard that encourages others to settle in your colony. Follow the steps below. When you complete each step, have your teacher initial it before you move to the next step.

_____ **Step 1: Review the roles.** After your teacher assigns your role, read the information below. Make sure everyone knows his or her responsibilities.

Historian: You will lead the group during Step 2 to make sure that everyone understands the key historical information about your colony.

Advertiser: You will lead the group during Step 3 to create a slogan and catchy statements that show your colony's outstanding features.

Graphic Artist: You will lead the group during Step 4 to create striking visuals that show key features of your colony on the billboard.

Salesperson: You will lead the group during Step 5 to create a memorable sales presentation to try to persuade others to settle in your colony.

_____ **Step 2: Learn about your colony.** Take turns reading aloud the information about your colony in Chapter 7 of your book. When you finish reading, the Historian should make sure that everyone in the group can complete the corresponding section of Reading Notes 7 from memory.

_____ **Step 3: Write a slogan and catchy statements for your billboard.** Your billboard must contain a slogan that summarizes your colony's most outstanding feature. For example, for the colony of Virginia, your group might write: *Make your dreams come true in the fertile soil of Virginia!* This slogan identifies one of Virginia's outstanding features: the availability of rich soil for farming. It also tries to persuade people to move to Virginia by suggesting that they could become wealthy there. After you have brainstormed some ideas, the Advertiser should write your group's slogan below.

Slogan:

Your billboard must also contain three catchy statements that describe other qualities of your colony, such as its geography or job opportunities. After you have brainstormed some ideas, the Advertiser should write the three catchy statements below.

Catchy statement 1:

Catchy statement 2

Catchy statement 3:

_____ **Step 4: Sketch visuals for your billboard.** Your billboard must contain four visuals that reinforce the ideas in your slogan and catchy statements. Your visuals should be simple and striking so that they can be easily seen from a distance. After you have brainstormed some ideas, the Graphic Artist should quickly sketch the four visuals in the space below.

_____ **Step 5: Brainstorm ideas for a sales presentation.** Your group's Salesperson will have one minute to present your billboard to the rest of the class. Make the presentation educational and entertaining. Use a memorable sales gimmick, such as distributing coupons or singing a musical jingle. In the space below, the Salesperson should outline the main ideas to include in the presentation.

_____ **Step 6: Create your billboard.** Work together to complete the final billboard on a large piece of butcher paper. Add creative touches, such as a decorative border and extra visuals, to make your billboard visually appealing.

_____ **Step 7: Rehearse the presentation.** The Salesperson should rehearse the sales presentation. Other group members should make sure that it is easy to follow, interesting to watch, and lasts no more than one minute.

Sample Billboard for the Virginia Colony

Make your dreams come true in the fertile soil of Virginia!

Experience the power of democracy by electing representatives to the House of Burgesses!

BALLOT ✗

Get rich growing tobacco on your own 50-acre plot of land!

There are numerous job opportunities in our booming economy!

bricklayers

shoemakers

tailors

Chapter 7 Assessment

Big Ideas

Fill in the circle next to the best answer.

1. The British included people from
   ○ A. Germany.
   ○ B. Holland.
   ○ C. Ireland.
   ○ D. Scotland.

2. The economies of the colonial regions differed because they had different
   ○ A. governments.
   ○ B. languages.
   ○ C. origins.
   ○ D. resources.

3. Plantations specialized in producing
   ○ A. fine food.
   ○ B. cash crops.
   ○ C. dairy cattle.
   ○ D. wood furniture.

4. Someone who agreed to work for an employer for a set period of time in order to pay off a debt was called
   ○ A. a slave.
   ○ B. an apprentice.
   ○ C. an assemblyman.
   ○ D. an indentured servant.

5. Massachusetts Bay was founded to protect
   ○ A. Baptists.
   ○ B. Catholics.
   ○ C. Puritans.
   ○ D. Quakers.

6. Why was Rhode Island founded?
   ○ A. as a trade center
   ○ B. for religious freedom
   ○ C. for large tobacco farms
   ○ D. as a place for the poor to settle

7. Why were the Quakers mistreated in England?
   ○ A. They refused to obey laws.
   ○ B. They often received special favors from the king.
   ○ C. They taught that people should overthrow kings by force.
   ○ D. They practiced a different religion from most English people.

8. Which of these was a disadvantage of Maryland as a place to settle?
   ○ A. Crops grew poorly.
   ○ B. There were no industries.
   ○ C. Mosquitoes spread disease.
   ○ D. There were no ports for ocean ships.

9. Why was Georgia founded?
   ○ A. to help poor people avoid being jailed for their debts
   ○ B. to trade with Spanish colonies
   ○ C. to raise taxes from new settlers
   ○ D. as a home for former slaves

Social Studies Skills

Use the map and your knowledge of social studies to complete the sentences. Write the word or phrase on the lines provided.

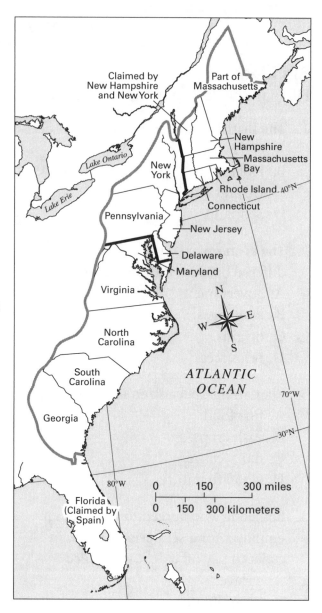

10. The British wanted the area they named New York so that British settlers in New England could _____

_____

_____.

11. Two colonies to the east of Lake Erie that offered jobs in the farming and iron mining industries were _____

and _____.

12. Just south of a colony established as a safe place for Quakers was the colony of

_____,

established by Lord Baltimore as a safe

place for _____

_____.

13. The colony of Georgia was founded in part to prevent an invasion of the British

colonies by _____ troops moving north from _____.

Reading Further

14. Some of the world's finest fishing grounds were off the coast of the _____

_____ colonial region, which included these four colonies:

_____, _____,

_____, and _____.

Show You Know

15. Look at the map on the previous page. Choose one colony from the New England Colonies, one from the Middle Colonies, and one from the Southern Colonies.

- On separate sheets of paper, draw a large map of each colony and write each colony's name.

- Under each map, write two sentences to explain why the colony was founded and how democratic its government was.

- On each map, follow these steps:
  a. Draw a symbol that indicates one feature of the geography of the area.
  b. Draw a symbol that indicates one job settlers did in the colony.
  c. Create a map key that shows the symbols and explains what they mean.

Chapter 8 Assessment

Big Ideas

Fill in the circle next to the best answer.

1. Which is the *best* example of a dilemma West Africans faced?
   - ○ A. how to visit nearby villages
   - ○ B. where to find camel caravans
   - ○ C. whether to trade people for guns
   - ○ D. when to sing songs and tell stories

2. Which of these was true of *most* West Africans in the 1500s?
   - ○ A. They spoke the same language.
   - ○ B. They were long-distance traders.
   - ○ C. They were captured and enslaved.
   - ○ D. They valued family and ancestors.

3. Where were *most* slaves in the West Indies and British North America put to work?
   - ○ A. gold and silver mines
   - ○ B. household kitchens
   - ○ C. grain and textile mills
   - ○ D. sugar and tobacco plantations

4. Slaves on a slave ship in the Middle Passage had a lot of
   - ○ A. living space.
   - ○ B. daily exercise.
   - ○ C. serious illness.
   - ○ D. successful revolts.

5. When Africans captured in the slave trade arrived in the American colonies, they were first
   - ○ A. reunited with family members.
   - ○ B. sold at scrambles or slave auctions.
   - ○ C. taught English so they could follow orders.
   - ○ D. told by the ship's captain where they would work.

6. What was an overseer's main job?
   - ○ A. to evaluate the price of slaves
   - ○ B. to supervise the work of slaves
   - ○ C. to teach slaves to use new tools
   - ○ D. to help slaves escape to the North

7. Why did some slaves pretend not to understand what they were told to do?
   - ○ A. It was a form of resistance.
   - ○ B. It spared their friends' feelings.
   - ○ C. It helped them learn English.
   - ○ D. It allowed them to buy freedom.

8. In general, which slaves had the hardest life?
   - ○ A. field workers
   - ○ B. house servants
   - ○ C. skilled carpenters
   - ○ D. kitchen gardeners

Social Studies Skills

Use the map and your knowledge of social studies to answer the questions.
Follow the instructions for each item.

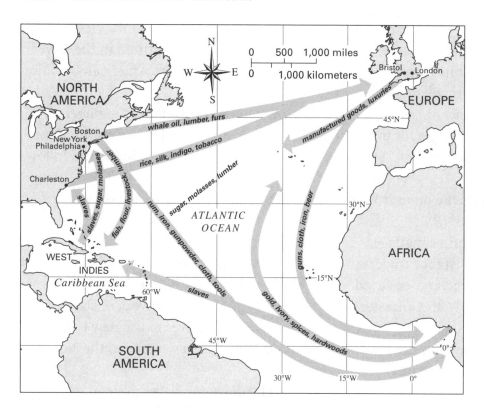

9. What is the name for the pattern of trade routes shown on the map?

10. Draw and label a dotted line along the route of the Middle Passage.

11. Use the information on the map to help you describe Great Britian's trade with Africa, the West Indies, and North America. Explain in your sentence the movement of people and goods.

Reading Further

12. On the map, draw a circle around the general area where Alex Haley learned about his family from a griot. Write the word *griot* in the circle.

13. On the map, draw a box around the general area where spirituals were a common form of cultural expression. Write the word *spirituals* in or near the box.

Show You Know

14. Write a story or song that an African slave in North America might have passed on to children or grandchildren, to teach them their family history. Show the experiences of the slave telling the story or song. Follow these guidelines:

- Explain the series of events that led to your being a slave in North America.

- Include a description of your life as a slave in North America.

- End with a message to be passed down through your family. It might be a message of hope, or a piece of advice. If the message is coded in symbols so that its meaning may not be obvious to a reader today, add a note explaining the meaning of the symbols.

Station A Labels

College of
William and
Mary

Station A Directions

The College of William and Mary, and Dame Schools

1. Trace your route to the College of William and Mary. On your Reading Notes map, draw a line from your last location to the College of William and Mary.

2. Examine Placard 9A. Discuss the question at the bottom of the placard.

3. Read Section 9.3 of your book. Record notes in Section 9.3 of your Reading Notes.

4. Complete one of the tasks described below. Do Task A if you are a girl and Task B if you are a boy.

Task A (for girls)

Suppose that you are a 10-year-old girl at a dame school. You are making a sewing sampler.

- Sit in the area labeled "Dame School."
- Take one sewing sampler and use a hole punch to punch holes around the border.
- Cut a length of yarn long enough to thread through all the holes of the sampler.
- Sew the sampler by threading the yarn through the holes.
- Put your name on the sampler and place the completed work on your teacher's desk.

Task B (for boys)

Suppose that you are a 10-year-old boy at the College of William and Mary. You are learning how to become a good colonial man.

- Sit in the area labeled "College of William and Mary."
- Be absolutely quiet while you do your work, or the colonial teacher will discipline you.
- Take a blank sheet of paper and write your name at the top.
- Using the ink and a stirring straw or toothpick as a pen, copy the following sentence: *In the Presence of Others Sing not to yourself with a humming Noise.* Write your name on the paper.
- Make sure your ink is dry and put your completed work on your teacher's desk.

5. Clean up the station. Make sure everything is back in its proper place before you leave.

Station A Material: Sewing Sampler

Rules of Civility and Decent Behaviour in Company and Conversation

1st   Every Action done in Company, ought to be with Some Sign of Respect, to those that are Present.

2nd When in Company, put not your Hands to any Part of the body, not usually Discovered.

3rd   Shew Nothing to your Friend that may affright him.

4th   In the Presence of Others Sing not to yourself with a humming Noise, nor Drum with your Fingers or Feet.

Station B Label

Shoemaker's Shop

Station B Directions

The Shoemaker's Shop

1. Trace your route to the shoemaker's shop. On your Reading Notes map, draw a line from your last location to the shoemaker's shop.

2. Examine Placard 9B. Discuss the question at the bottom of the placard.

3. Read Section 9.4 of your book. Record notes in Section 9.4 of your Reading Notes.

4. With your partner, act out the roles of the shoemaker and a customer.
   - Have the customer enter the shoemaker's shop, greet the shoemaker, and request a custom-made pair of boots.
   - Have the customer remove a shoe and place his or her foot on one of the thick pieces of paper or card stock.
   - Have the shoemaker use a crayon to trace the customer's foot on the card stock.
   - Have the shoemaker use scissors to cut out the "sole," and then use a crayon to write the customer's name on it. Also, write the color of boots the customer wants.
   - Switch roles and complete a sole for the new customer.
   - Set the labeled soles aside so that the journeyman or apprentice can make the boots later.

5. Clean up the station. Make sure everything is back in its proper place before you leave.

Station C Label

Station C Directions

Raleigh Tavern

1. Trace your route to Raleigh Tavern. On your Reading Notes map, draw a line from your last location to Raleigh Tavern.

2. Examine Placard 9C. Discuss the question at the bottom of the placard.

3. Read Section 9.5 of your book. Record notes in Section 9.5 of your Reading Notes.

4. Complete the task described below.
   - Act out arriving at Raleigh Tavern and ordering a delicious meal of peanut soup and shepherd's pie.
   - Sit with your partner to play *The Royall and Most Pleasant Game of the Goose.* Choose a token and follow the directions to play the game.

5. Clean up the station. Make sure everything is back in its proper place before you leave.

The Royall and Most Pleasant Game of the Goose

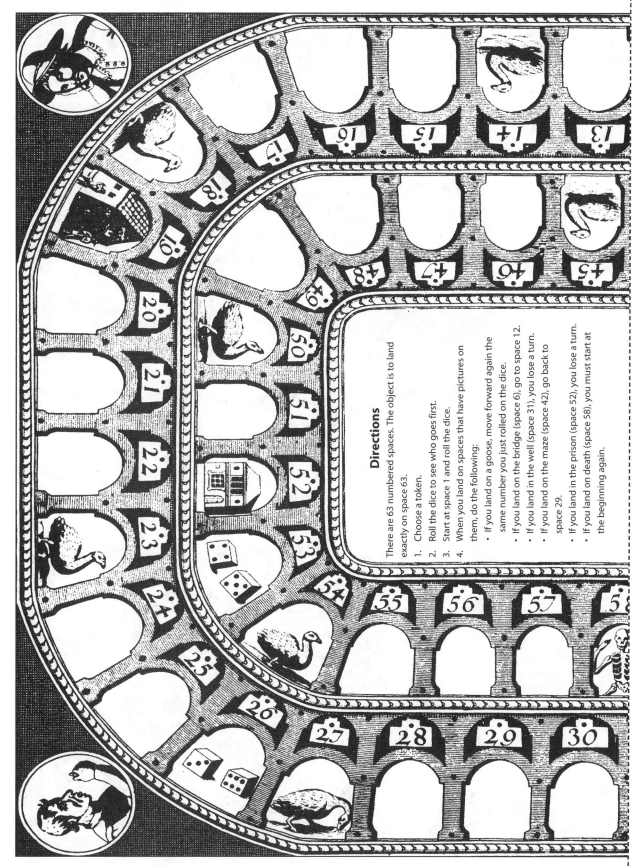

Directions

There are 63 numbered spaces. The object is to land exactly on space 63.

1. Choose a token.
2. Roll the dice to see who goes first.
3. Start at space 1 and roll the dice.
4. When you land on spaces that have pictures on them, do the following:

 • If you land on a goose, move forward again the same number you just rolled on the dice.
 • If you land on the bridge (space 6), go to space 12.
 • If you land in the well (space 31), you lose a turn.
 • If you land on the maze (space 42), go back to space 29.
 • If you land in the prison (space 52), you lose a turn.
 • If you land on death (space 58), you must start at the beginning again.

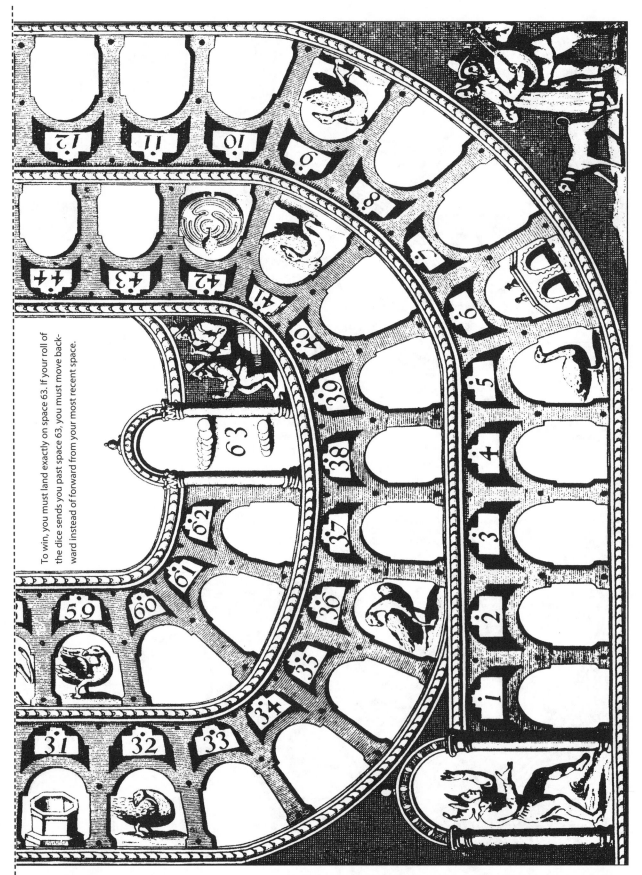

To win, you must land exactly on space 63. If your roll of the dice sends you past space 63, you must move backward instead of forward from your most recent space.

Station D Label

Governor's Palace

Life in Colonial Williamsburg **69**

Station D Directions

The Governor's Palace

1. Trace your route to the Governor's Palace. On your Reading Notes map, draw a line from your last location to the Governor's Palace.

2. Examine Placard 9D. Discuss the question at the bottom of the placard.

3. Read Section 9.6 of your book. Stop reading at the heading "Actions of Virginia's Royal Governor." Record notes in Section 9.6 of your Reading Notes.

4. Complete the task described below.
   - Suppose that you are the royal governor of Virginia. You have the power to approve or reject certain government actions.
   - Take one copy of each of the three Government Actions and read them. Decide whether you want to approve each one.
   - If you approve a Government Action, sign the document and stamp it with the royal seal.
   - If you reject a Government Action, do not sign or stamp it.
   - Put approved Government Actions in one pile. Put rejected Government Actions in another pile.

5. Learn the actual outcome of these Government Actions. Read "Actions of Virginia's Royal Governor" on the second page of Section 9.6 in your book. Compare the actual outcome with your decision on each of the Government Actions.

6. Clean up the station. Make sure everything is back in its proper place before you leave.

Government Actions for Governor's Review

Royal Stamp

Government Action 1: Assembly Bill for a Lighthouse at Cape Henry

In the past 10 years, many sea vessels, or ships, have been stranded near Cape Henry. Therefore, it is hereby established that the Virginia government will build a lighthouse at Cape Henry. The lighthouse will surely secure safe trade among sea vessels in this great land.

_____
Signature of the Royal Governor

Royal Stamp

Government Action 2: Assembly Bill for Voting in the Colony of Virginia

No slave or free black man shall vote in elections.

No woman shall vote. In addition, no white man without property shall vote.

No person shall vote who is not a member of the Anglican Church.

_____
Signature of the Royal Governor

Royal Stamp

Government Action 3: Request for Pardon for a Teenaged Pirate

This request is to pardon, or release from punishment, John Vidal. Vidal is a 16-year-old convicted pirate, or robber of ships at sea. Mr. Vidal has admitted stealing from the people of Virginia. His crime is punishable by death. The young Mr. John Vidal claims that he "never intended to go a-pirating." "With a weeping heart," he has begged for mercy. This pardon states that young Mr. John Vidal will not serve a death penalty for his admitted crimes.

_____
Signature of the Royal Governor

Station E Label

Station E Directions

Slave Quarters at a Tobacco Plantation

1. Trace your route to the slave quarters at the tobacco plantation. On your Reading Notes map, draw a line from your last location to the slave quarters.

2. Examine Placard 9E. Discuss the question at the bottom of the placard.

3. Read Section 9.7 of your book. Record notes in Section 9.7 of your Reading Notes.

4. Complete the task described below.
   - Play CD Track 2, "Juba."
   - Listen to the narrator to learn how to make rhythm sounds and how to sing along with "Juba," a call-and-response song. Follow his directions.
   - When the song is over, stop the CD player.
   - Before leaving the slave quarters, discuss these questions with your partner: *What do you think was the purpose of this song? Why would enslaved people sing this song together?*

5. Clean up the station. Make sure everything is back in its proper place before you leave.

Station F Labels

Station F Directions

Bruton Parish Church

1. Trace your route to Bruton Parish Church. On your Reading Notes map, draw a line from your last location to Bruton Parish Church.

2. Examine Placard 9F. Discuss the question at the bottom of the placard.

3. Read Section 9.8 of your book. Record notes in Section 9.8 of your Reading Notes.

4. Complete the task described below.
   - Suppose that you are a Virginian standing outside Bruton Parish Church on a Sunday morning. Like all Virginians, you are required by law to attend church. Be quiet and respectful while at this station.
   - Choose a role card and read it. Do not enter the church yet.
   - Read the announcements posted on the bulletin board outside the church.
   - Take a sheet of paper from the floor and write a short announcement as if you were the person on the role card. Post it on the bulletin board on the wall outside the church.
   - Enter the church. Use your role card and information from Section 9.8 of your book to find the correct place to sit.
   - After you sit down, check the seating chart at your place to make sure you are seated in the correct location.
   - Sit quietly in the church for two minutes. Imagine what the person on your role card would be thinking about if she or he were in church.
   - When you leave the church, be quiet and respectful. Put your role card back where you found it.

5. Clean up the station. Make sure everything is back in its proper place before you leave.

Station F Material: Sample Community Announcements

Baptism

There will be a special baptism service next Sunday for Helen Alice Windsor, daughter of George and Alice Windsor.

Slave named Henry ran away last Saturday. Reward for his capture and return.

Mr. Jason Randolph

Station F Material: Role Cards for Parishioners

Role Card 1

Your name is Walter Geddy. You own a large tobacco plantation and are one of the richest men in town. You have seven daughters and two sons.

Role Card 2

Your name is Martha Geddy. You are married to Walter Geddy, who owns a large tobacco plantation and is one of the richest men in town. You have seven daughters and two sons.

Role Card 3

Your name is William Davis. You are an enslaved African American. You live on the Geddy family plantation.

Role Card 4

Your name is Sarah Johnson. Your husband owns the shoemaker's shop in town. You are not rich but are considered middle class. You recently had a baby girl.

Role Card 5

Your name is Bob Wilson. You are a journeyman carpenter, but you lost your job several weeks ago. You have been trying to do odd jobs so you can support your family.

Role Card 6

Your name is Thomas Cleary. You are a student at the College of William and Mary. You are trying to earn extra money by tutoring younger students at their homes.

Station F Material: Church Seating Chart

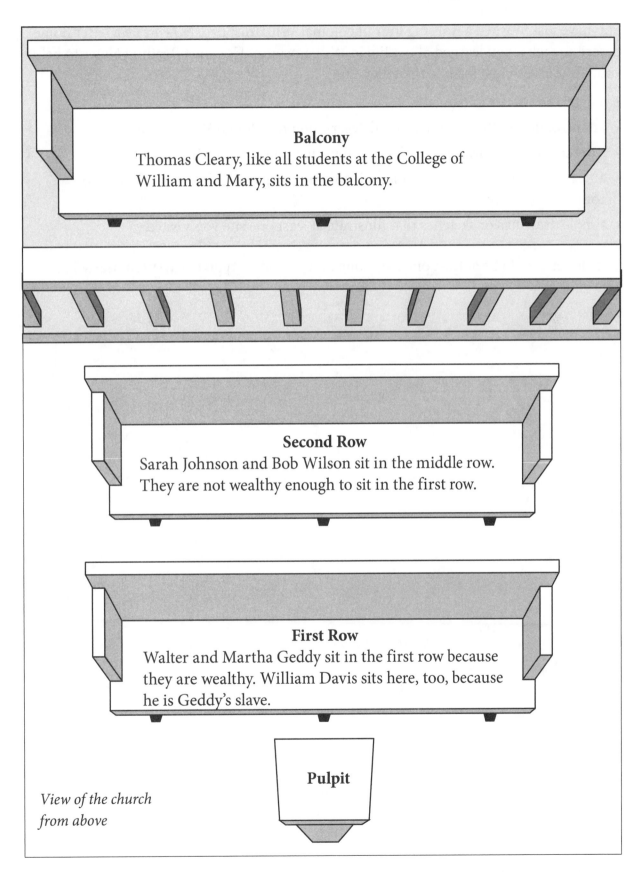

Balcony
Thomas Cleary, like all students at the College of William and Mary, sits in the balcony.

Second Row
Sarah Johnson and Bob Wilson sit in the middle row. They are not wealthy enough to sit in the first row.

First Row
Walter and Martha Geddy sit in the first row because they are wealthy. William Davis sits here, too, because he is Geddy's slave.

Pulpit

View of the church from above

Writing a Letter About Colonial Williamsburg

You have just finished a walking tour of colonial Williamsburg. Now write a letter home describing what you learned about life in Williamsburg. Use your Reading Notes to help you. Your letter must include the following:

- a date and proper greeting
- an introduction that gives a general description of colonial Williamsburg
- a description of at least three places you visited on your walking tour
- an explanation of how life in colonial Williamsburg compares with life in your community today
- simple drawings or sketches that illustrate at least one site you visited

Your letter should be at least one page long and should be typed or written neatly in ink.

Chapter 9 Assessment

Big Ideas
Fill in the circle next to the best answer.

1. Which of these best describes colonial Williamsburg?
   ○ A. closed to outside visitors
   ○ B. wealthy all-white community
   ○ C. center of education and culture
   ○ D. far from the capital of Virginia

2. What happened at the capitol building?
   ○ A. The king visited there.
   ○ B. Lawmakers met there.
   ○ C. The governor lived there.
   ○ D. Men and women voted there.

3. Where did some girls in Williamsburg learn to read?
   ○ A. dame schools
   ○ B. classes run by a minister
   ○ C. College of William and Mary
   ○ D. schools to train Anglican priests

4. In which of these buildings might a craftsman be most likely to teach apprentices a trade?
   ○ A. slave quarters
   ○ B. Raleigh Tavern
   ○ C. shoemaker's shop
   ○ D. Bruton Parish Church

5. Why did colonial leaders go to the Raleigh Tavern?
   ○ A. to visit their families
   ○ B. to discuss business and politics
   ○ C. to hear inspiring sermons
   ○ D. to make laws for the colony

6. When leaders of Virginia discussed politics, what did they talk about?
   ○ A. agriculture
   ○ B. travel
   ○ C. family
   ○ D. government

7. Who chose the governor of the royal colony of Virginia?
   ○ A. the king
   ○ B. the voters
   ○ C. the lawmakers
   ○ D. the church members

8. What was the official religion of Virginia?
   ○ A. Anglican
   ○ B. Baptist
   ○ C. Catholic
   ○ D. Puritan

Reading Further

9. How did religious services after the Great Awakening differ from services before that time?
   ○ A. People followed rules.
   ○ B. People met in churches.
   ○ C. People showed emotions.
   ○ D. People listened to ministers.

10. Which teaching of the Great Awakening changed colonists' ideas?
    ○ A. Singing is a sin.
    ○ B. People should be kind.
    ○ C. Kings should be overthrown.
    ○ D. All people are important.

Social Studies Skills

Below is an excerpt from a contract that will make a young man named John Stevens an apprentice to a tailor named George Charleton. Read the document. Then answer the questions.

> *Witnesseth that the said John Stevens with the advice and consent of his Mother Anne Stevens doth put himself an Apprentice to the said George Charleton to learn the Trade, art, and Mistery of a Taylor* and with him after the manner of an Apprentice to serve till he arrives to the Age of Twenty-one Years . . . [George Charleton promises to provide] Meat Drink Washing Lodging & Cloathing during the Said Term and to Teach him to Read & Write . . .*
>
> *Williamsburg, 1784*
>
> * *Tailor:* someone who makes or mends clothing

11. When John Stevens is an apprentice, what are two things his master will teach him?

12. When will John Stevens finish his time as an apprentice?

13 What will he most likely do after his apprenticeship? Explain your reasoning.

14. What is the most likely reason he needs his mother's permission to be an apprentice?

Show You Know

15. Listen to the call-and-response song "Juba" on CD Track 2. This song was sung by enslaved African Americans and is about the leftover food they were given to eat. On a separate sheet of paper, write new song lyrics (words) to the song "Juba." Follow these guidelines:

A. Choose one of the following singers and topics:
  - an apprentice in the shoemaker's shop, who sings about his work there
  - a student, who sings about education for boys and girls in Williamsburg
  - the royal governor, who sings about what it is like to govern Virginia
  - a member of Bruton Parish Church, who sings about religion in Williamsburg
  - the owner of Raleigh Tavern, who sings about things that happen at the tavern

B. Write a new title for the song.

C. Write at least six call-and-response lines (each call and response counts as one line) that describe interesting information from the singer's point of view.

PTA Memo

To: Teachers
From: Parent-Teacher Association
Re: Class parties

This memo is to inform you that a class party planned by students at a nearby school caused a number of problems that concerned parents. The problems include the following:

- Students missed hours of instructional time while they planned and held the party.
- The site students selected was unsafe; uninvited older students disrupted the party.
- Several students were injured during games involving physical contact, such as tackle football and dodgeball.
- Some students complained afterward about stomachaches caused by the consumption of junk food.
- The party costs were in excess of school policy.

Therefore, the PTA has decided to set specific guidelines for all class parties. From this time forward, all parties must conform to these guidelines:

- For educational purposes, all class parties will be held during lunch period on Tuesdays, Wednesdays, or Thursdays, for no more than 30 minutes.
- For safety reasons, all class parties will be held in the classroom.
- For safety reasons, only approved games, such as Pin-the-Tail-on-the-Donkey and Beanbag Toss, will be allowed.
- For health reasons, food or drink with a high sugar content, such as soft drinks, cakes, and candy, will not be served. Water, fruit juices, and vegetable sticks are acceptable alternatives.
- For financial reasons, all students must pay $1.00 to help fund the party. Students who do not bring money may not participate.

Illustrations for Reading Notes 10

Chapter 10 Assessment

Big Ideas

Fill in the circle next to the best answer.

1. Which of these was an outcome of the French and Indian War?
   - ○ A. British territory was reduced.
   - ○ B. France defeated Great Britain.
   - ○ C. The British went deeply into debt.
   - ○ D. Relations between the colonists and Great Britain improved.

2. What was the purpose of the Proclamation of 1763?
   - ○ A. to protect the colonists
   - ○ B. to punish the settlers
   - ○ C. to make money for the war
   - ○ D. to reward American Indians

3. Which part of the British government passed acts?
   - ○ A. Parliament
   - ○ B. the royal family
   - ○ C. the British Congress
   - ○ D. the House of Burgesses

4. Which of these laws made colonists provide British soldiers with food, transportation, and housing?
   - ○ A. the Stamp Act
   - ○ B. the Quartering Act
   - ○ C. the Coercive Acts
   - ○ D. the Proclamation of 1763

5. How did colonists react to the Stamp Act?
   - ○ A. ignored it
   - ○ B. considered it fair
   - ○ C. protested until it was repealed
   - ○ D. disliked it but went along with it

6. The Townshend Acts taxed several goods that the colonies imported, or
   - ○ A. tried to sell in other countries.
   - ○ B. manufactured for use at home.
   - ○ C. raised on farms and plantations.
   - ○ D. brought into the colonies for sale.

7. Which did not feed the anger that led to the Boston Massacre?
   - ○ A. The Quartering Act
   - ○ B. The Stamp Act
   - ○ C. The Townshend Acts
   - ○ D. The Boston Tea Party

8. What did the colonists call the laws that were passed to punish them after the Boston Tea Party?
   - ○ A. the Boston Massacre
   - ○ B. the Intolerable Acts
   - ○ C. the Quartering Act
   - ○ D. the Stamp Act

Social Studies Skills

Look at the illustrations. Then answer the questions.

9. Describe how the parent's action is like Great Britain's action in putting a tax on goods the colonists enjoyed.

10. Describe how the child's response is a form of boycott.

11. Which British law does this illustration refer to?

12. How might the child feel like treating the dogs? Compare that reaction with the way some colonists behaved.

Reading Further

13. In the two situations shown in the illustrations, which character would King George III most likely have agreed with? Explain your answer.

Show You Know

14. Make up and draw an illustrated metaphor. Follow these guidelines::

- The metaphor should relate to one historical event or development described in this chapter.

- The characters' words and actions should illustrate at least one factor in the tensions between Great Britain and the colonies.

- One or two sentences below the illustration should explain the point the metaphor is making about the relationship between Great Britain and the colonies.

Preparing for the Panel Debate

Your group will bring to life a historical figure. This figure will debate whether the American colonies should declare independence from Great Britain. Follow the steps below to prepare your historical figure for the debate. Have your teacher initial each step when your group completes it.

_____ **Step 1: Review your role.** Your teacher will assign you a role. Then you should read the information below. Make sure you clearly understand what you have to do.

Public Relations Agent: You will lead the group during Step 2. Then you will write a statement to introduce your historical figure during the panel debate.

Actor: You will lead the group during Step 3. Then you will bring the historical figure to life during the panel debate.

Investigative Reporter: You will lead the group during Step 4. Then you will direct questions to your historical figure's opponents during the panel debate.

Costume Designer: You will lead the group during Step 5. Then you will create a costume and props for your historical figure to use during the panel debate.

_____ **Step 2: Learn about your historical figure.** Take turns reading aloud the information about your historical figure in Chapter 11 of your book. When you finish reading, have the Public Relations Agent record answers to these questions:

1. What occupation(s) did your historical figure hold during the American Revolution?

2. What are three important details to remember about your historical figure's personal life?

3. How would your historical figure answer when asked, "Should the American colonies declare independence?"

4. What actions did your historical figure take for or against independence?

_____ **Step 3: Prepare your Actor.** Your group's Actor will have to explain his or her position during the panel debate. Think of three arguments your Actor could use to support his or her answer to the question, "Should the American colonies declare independence?" Have the Actor record your answers below.

Help your Actor think of three different ways he or she might act or behave during the debate to reflect your historical figure's personality. For example, he or she might shout to show anger or roll his or her eyes to show disagreement. Have the Actor record your ideas below. (Look for ideas about how your figure would look and act in your book.)

_____ **Step 4: Prepare questions for your historical figure's opponents on the panel.** During the panel debate, Investigative Reporters will be asking questions of the other historical figures. To prepare, read the three sections about your opponents in your book. Then have the Investigative Reporter write at least one question for each opponent. For example, if your historical figure is a Patriot, you might ask Loyalist Thomas Hutchinson, "Why do you enforce British laws that are unfair to the colonists?" Record your questions below.

Opponent 1:
Question:

Opponent 2:
Question:

Opponent 3:
Question:

_____ **Step 5: Prepare materials for the panel debate.** To bring your figure to life during the panel debate, the Costume Designer will make sure each of the following tasks is completed:

- **Actor** cuts out and decorates the mask so that it looks realistic. Make sure that he or she can breathe, see, and speak through it.

- **Public Relations Agent** writes a 30-second introductory statement that includes your historical figure's name, occupation, accomplishments, and views on independence.

- **Costume Designer** gathers appropriate materials for your historical figure to wear and props for him or her to hold during the panel discussion. (Look for ideas in your book.)

- **Investigative Reporter** designs a nameplate that includes the name of your historical figure in large letters, a slogan, and an illustration that represents your figure's viewpoints. Here is an example of what a nameplate for George Washington might look like:

George Washington
"Our First President and the Father of Our Country"
☆☆☆

_____ **Step 6: Rehearse for the panel debate.** As you rehearse, make sure that

- the Public Relations Agent can deliver the introductory statement clearly.

- the Actor speaks clearly and dramatically and can explain his or her views on the issue of whether or not the American colonies should declare independence from Great Britain.

- the Costume Designer and the Investigative Reporter prepare the Actor for questions that opponents on the panel might ask.

Mask of Thomas Hutchinson

Mask of Jonathan Boucher

Mask of Lord Dunmore

Mask of Benjamin Franklin

Mask of Mercy Otis Warren

Mask of Samuel Adams

Illustrations for Reading Notes 11

Chapter 11 Assessment

Big Ideas

Fill in the circle next to the best answer.

1. Which colonists were called Patriots?
   ○ A. those who obeyed the laws
   ○ B. those who were willing to fight
   ○ C. those who wanted independence
   ○ D. those who were loyal to the king

2. Rich landowners, governors, and religious leaders were often
   ○ A. Loyalists.
   ○ B. neutral.
   ○ C. Patriots.
   ○ D. red coats.

3. Why did many colonists boycott tea and paper?
   ○ A. to punish the storekeepers
   ○ B. to protest taxes on those items
   ○ C. to save money for future needs
   ○ D. to make their own goods at home

4. Which of the following colonists would most likely have agreed with this statement: "The king of England knows what is best for the colonies"?
   ○ A. Thomas Hutchinson
   ○ B. Benjamin Franklin
   ○ C. Samuel Adams
   ○ D. a neutral colonist

5. Traitors are people who act against
   ○ A. common sense.
   ○ B. the Patriots in the colonies.
   ○ C. the public good.
   ○ D. their own country.

6. Benjamin Franklin tried to persuade the British Parliament to
   ○ A. treat the colonies fairly.
   ○ B. free enslaved Africans.
   ○ C. give the colonies independence.
   ○ D. give women colonists more rights.

7. Which of the following colonists would most likely have agreed with this statement: "British laws and taxes are unfair to the colonies"?
   ○ A. Jonathan Boucher
   ○ B. Lord Dunmore
   ○ C. Mercy Otis Warren
   ○ D. a neutral colonist

Reading Further

8. A lawyer said Patrick Henry had committed treason because Henry
   ○ A. called the king a tyrant.
   ○ B. argued against a minister.
   ○ C. defended a law of Virginia.
   ○ D. dressed improperly in court.

9. Which famous words are from a speech by Patrick Henry?
   ○ A. "We the people"
   ○ B. "All men are created equal."
   ○ C. "You have a duty to be loyal."
   ○ D. "Give me liberty or give me death."

Social Studies Skills

The pie chart represents the views of 80 colonists in one New Jersey village in 1775 on whether or not to declare independence from Great Britain. Use the chart and your knowledge of social studies to answer the questions below.

Villagers' Political Views

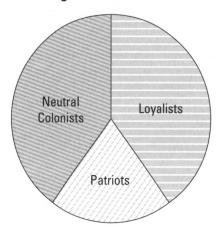

10. Based on the chart, which of the three groups has the least support?

11. If the villagers took a vote at the meeting and none of the neutral colonists voted, which side won the vote?

12. If the villagers took a vote and all the neutral colonists voted on the side of the Patriots, which side won?

13. What argument might the neutral colonists in the village use to try to persuade the others that the village should remain neutral?

14. Do you think that this village is similar to or different from how most of the colonies viewed independence? Explain your answer.

Show You Know

15. Write a short play. The play should have these three characters:
    - a Loyalist
    - a Patriot
    - a neutral colonist

    The play should also have:
    - a setting in the American colonies.
    - a situation that requires the neutral colonist to support the Patriots or the Loyalists.

    Have the Loyalist and the Patriot each try to influence the neutral colonist's decision.

Glossary for the Declaration of Independence

There are some difficult words and phrases in the Declaration of Independence. Below are definitions for these words and phrases. Use these definitions to help you understand each excerpt. On Reading Notes 12 in your Interactive Student Notebook, rewrite each excerpt so that it is easier to understand.

Excerpt 1
dissolve: end
bonds: ties
impel: force

Excerpt 2
self-evident: obvious
endow: provide
unalienable: not to be taken away

Excerpt 3
secure: make safe
institute: establish
derive: receive
just: legal
consent: agreement
alter: change
abolish: get rid of

Excerpt 4
usurpation: illegal seizure of power
in direct object: the goal of
tyranny: government by an unjust ruler
submit: present for judgment
candid: fair

Excerpt 5
solemnly: seriously
absolve: free from
allegiance: loyalty
British crown: British king

Preparing Skits for the Declaration of Independence

Your group must prepare a skit to bring an excerpt from the Declaration of Independence to life. Follow these steps to create your skit:

_____ **Step 1: Brainstorm ideas about how to bring the excerpt to life.** As you review the excerpt from the Declaration of Independence, make note of how you can accurately bring the excerpt to life in a one-minute skit.

_____ **Step 2: Prepare props and costumes.** Your presentation must include costumes and props. Find or create simple props—such as textbooks, rulers, erasers, and chairs—to use in your skit.

_____ **Step 3: Agree on what each actor will say.** Decide what each person will say, and write a brief script on a sheet of paper.

_____ **Step 4: Rehearse your skit.** You must be able to perform your skit in one minute or less. As you rehearse, make sure

- the skit flows smoothly.
- costumes and props are used in the presentation.
- group members are positioned properly and know what movements they will make during the skit.
- lines are read clearly and dramatically.
- the skit accurately captures the meaning of the excerpt.

Chapter 12 Assessment

Big Ideas

Fill in the circle next to the best answer.

1. At the beginning of the American Revolution, British troops fought against
    - ○ A. a strong central army.
    - ○ B. knights on horseback.
    - ○ C. hired foreign soldiers.
    - ○ D. colonial militias and Minutemen.

2. An important task facing the Second Continental Congress was to
    - ○ A. organize the colonies for war.
    - ○ B. shut down the Continental army.
    - ○ C. find ways to make the king happy.
    - ○ D. make treaties with American Indian tribes.

3. The booklet *Common Sense* persuaded American colonists to
    - ○ A. want independence.
    - ○ B. forget about politics.
    - ○ C. ask for help from the king.
    - ○ D. remain loyal to Great Britain.

4. The purpose of the Declaration of Independence was to
    - ○ A. put an end to slavery.
    - ○ B. offer the king one last chance.
    - ○ C. ask for money to solve problems.
    - ○ D. explain why the colonies should be free.

5. The main writer of the Declaration of Independence was
    - ○ A. John Adams.
    - ○ B. Benjamin Franklin.
    - ○ C. Thomas Jefferson.
    - ○ D. George Washington.

6. Colonists rang bells and lit bonfires for the Declaration because they were
    - ○ A. angry.
    - ○ B. excited.
    - ○ C. worried.
    - ○ D. surprised.

7. Which of these ideas was in the Declaration of Independence?
    - ○ A. Women and men are equal.
    - ○ B. All rights can be taken away.
    - ○ C. Great Britain has ruled the colonies unfairly.
    - ○ D. People should obey governments even when they are unfair.

Reading Further

8. Although Thomas Jefferson believed in equality, he still
    - ○ A. was poor.
    - ○ B. owned slaves.
    - ○ C. respected the king.
    - ○ D. thought women should vote.

Social Studies Skills

Read the excerpts below from the Declaration of Independence. Answer the questions.

> **A.** I.   When in the Course of human events it becomes necessary for one people to dissolve the political bands which have connected them with another, . . . a decent respect to the opinions of mankind requires that they should declare the causes which impel them to the separation.
>
> **B.** II.   We hold these truths to be self-evident, that all men are created equal, that they are endowed by their Creator with certain unalienable Rights, that among these are life, liberty and the pursuit of happiness.
>
> **C.** III. That to secure these rights, Governments are instituted among Men, deriving their just powers from the consent of the governed. That whenever any Form of Government becomes destructive of these ends, it is the Right of the People to alter or to abolish it, and to institute new Government.
>
> **D.** IV. The history of the present King of Great Britain is a history of repeated injuries and usurpations, all having, in direct object, the establishment of an absolute Tyranny over these States. To prove this, let facts be submitted to a candid world.
>
> **E.** V.   (We) solemnly publish and declare, That these United Colonies are, and of right ought to be Free and Independent States; that they are Absolved from all Allegiance to the British Crown, and that all political connection between them and that State of Great Britain, is and ought to be totally dissolved.

9. What "political bands" are the writers referring to in Paragraph A?

10. Look at Paragraph B. List three rights the Declaration says cannot be taken away.
    a.

    b.

    c.

11. According to Paragraph C, where do governments get their power?

12. According to Paragraph D, what was the king's purpose in taking away the colonists' rights?

13. Read Paragraph E. When does the Declaration say the colonies would be independent?

Show You Know

14. Create a thought bubble outside the image for each person labeled in the painting below. In each bubble, write one or two sentences that describe what that person might be thinking and feeling at this moment. Include and underline each of the following in at least one of the thought bubbles:

- Second Continental Congress
- Declaration of Independence
- *Common Sense*
- treason
- British king

Chapter 13 Assessment

Big Ideas
Fill in the circle next to the best answer.

1. Overthrowing one government and replacing it with another is called
   - ○ A. a strategy.
   - ○ B. a turnover.
   - ○ C. a revolution.
   - ○ D. an enlistment.

2. The Continental army was made up of
   - ○ A. mercenaries.
   - ○ B. officers.
   - ○ C. privateers.
   - ○ D. volunteers.

3. Thousands of American Indians fought for Great Britain because the British had
   - ○ A. trapped furs for them.
   - ○ B. given them food supplies.
   - ○ C. offered to free them after the war.
   - ○ D. restricted settlement on their land.

4. Why was it hard for the British to replace troops and supplies?
   - ○ A. Their homeland was far away.
   - ○ B. They made the Loyalists angry.
   - ○ C. Parliament would not pay them.
   - ○ D. Their army was poorly trained.

5. Which phrase describes a tactic of the Continental army?
   - ○ A. desire to win
   - ○ B. surprise attacks
   - ○ C. food and supplies
   - ○ D. control of key cities

6. How did some allies help the Continental army?
   - ○ A. supplied soldiers and warships
   - ○ B. borrowed money from colonists
   - ○ C. joined up with American Indians
   - ○ D. captured Canada from the British

7. Why is the Battle of Saratoga considered a turning point?
   - ○ A. The British agreed to end the war.
   - ○ B. The colonial victory persuaded France to give more help.
   - ○ C. Washington defeated the German mercenaries.
   - ○ D. The British government took Florida from Spain.

8. Which of these was not an outcome of the Treaty of Paris?
   - ○ A. All slaves in the army were freed.
   - ○ B. Thousands of Loyalists fled.
   - ○ C. The new nation got huge amounts of land.
   - ○ D. Great Britain recognized the United States.

Reading Further
9. Which of these was part of the home front?
   - ○ A. a battlefield
   - ○ B. a family farm
   - ○ C. a warship at sea
   - ○ D. an army camp

Social Studies Skills

Use this painting of the Continental army at Valley Forge to answer the questions below.

10. At what time of year does this scene take place? How can you tell?

11. Describe something about the soldiers' clothing that adds to their discomfort.

12. List two ways in which the men are trying to keep warm.

13. Why might the painter have felt proud of the Americans in this painting?

Show You Know

14. Suppose that you are one of these people in the American Revolution:

_____ a soldier in the British army

_____ a soldier in the Continental army

_____ a woman helping the colonial soldiers

Put a check mark on the line beside the person you choose. Now, write a letter home to your family. Your letter should include

- an explanation of why you are on this side.
- an example of your day-to-day experience in the war.
- at least one advantage you see for your side.
- at least one disadvantage or hardship you see for your side.

Constitutional Power Cards

Power Card 1: Legislative Branch

Congress can write bills, or proposals for new laws.

Power Card 2: Legislative Branch

If the president vetoes (rejects) a bill, Congress can overrule the veto. It needs a two-thirds majority to do this.

Power Card 3: Legislative Branch

Congress can declare war.

Power Card 4: Legislative Branch

The House of Representatives can impeach government officials, including the president and federal judges.

Power Card 5: Legislative Branch

The Senate must approve the president's choices for Supreme Court justices and certain other key jobs.

Power Card 6: Legislative Branch

Two thirds of the Senate must approve any treaty between the United States and another country.

Power Card 7: Executive Branch

The president must sign or veto (reject) all bills passed by Congress.

Power Card 8: Executive Branch

The president can use the State of the Union speech to suggest ideas for new laws.

Power Card 9: Executive Branch

The president can call Congress together for a special session.

Power Card 10: Executive Branch

The president can grant pardons (release from punishment) to people guilty of federal crimes.

Power Card 11: Executive Branch

The president can nominate Supreme Court justices and other important officials.

Power Card 12: Executive Branch

The president can sign treaties with other nations.

Power Card 13: Executive Branch

The president is commander in chief of the nation's armed forces.

Power Card 14: Judicial Branch

The judicial branch can reject laws that are unconstitutional.

Power Card 15: Judicial Branch

The judicial branch can reject treaties that are unconstitutional.

Power Card 16: Judicial Branch

The federal courts can settle disagreements about what a law means.

Power Card 17: Judicial Branch

The chief justice acts as the judge during an impeachment trial in the Senate.

Illustrations for Constitutional Power Cards

Constitutional Situations

Situation 1 Scientists warn that a huge meteor is headed directly for the United States. Many people have ideas about how to deal with this national emergency. What can the government do?

Power Card 9: Executive Branch

Senators   Representatives

The president can call Congress together for a special session.

Situation 2 A key government official is convicted of taking a bribe. The official is humiliated and resigns from his job. Because the official had served the country well for more than 30 years, government leaders do not want him to go to jail. What can the government do?

Power Card 10: Executive Branch

The president can grant pardons (release from punishment) to people guilty of federal crimes.

Situation 3 According to law, you are not permitted to harass people because of their gender or race. This means you cannot trouble people repeatedly because they are male or female, or because of their skin color. However, the law is not clear on what words or actions are considered harassment. What can the government do?

Power Card 16: Judicial Branch

This law means...

The federal courts can settle disagreements about what a law means.

Situation 4 People want to know about new ideas the president has for solving national problems. What can the government do?

Power Card 8: Executive Branch

My ideas for new laws...

The president can use the State of the Union speech to suggest ideas for new laws.

Situation 5 The president is accused of committing serious crimes. What can the government do?

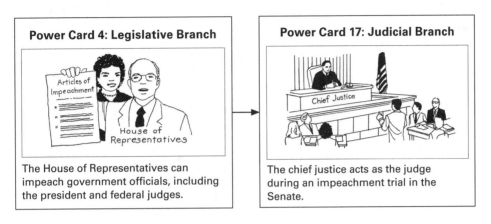

Power Card 4: Legislative Branch

The House of Representatives can impeach government officials, including the president and federal judges.

Power Card 17: Judicial Branch

The chief justice acts as the judge during an impeachment trial in the Senate.

Situation 6 A Supreme Court justice retires and must be replaced. What can the government do?

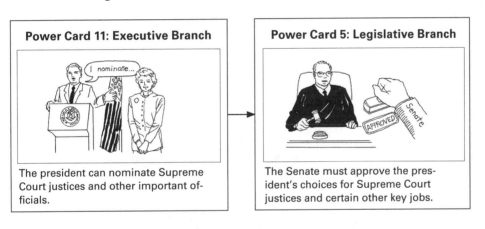

Power Card 11: Executive Branch

The president can nominate Supreme Court justices and other important officials.

Power Card 5: Legislative Branch

The Senate must approve the president's choices for Supreme Court justices and certain other key jobs.

Situation 7 Another country attacks the United States. What can the government do?

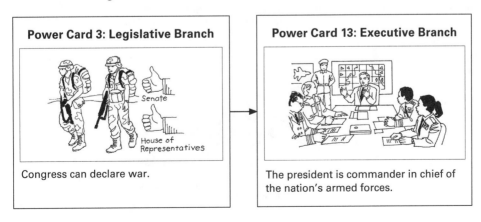

Power Card 3: Legislative Branch

Congress can declare war.

Power Card 13: Executive Branch

The president is commander in chief of the nation's armed forces.

Situation 8 A country wants to negotiate a treaty with the United States. They want to be military allies, or friends, of our nation. What can the government do?

Situation 9 The government learns that most citizens want it to spend more money on public schools. What can the government do?

Power Card 12: Executive Branch

The president can sign treaties with other nations.

Power Card 6: Legislative Branch

Two thirds of the Senate must approve any treaty between the United States and another country.

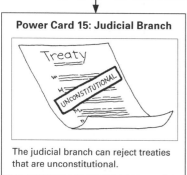

Power Card 15: Judicial Branch

The judicial branch can reject treaties that are unconstitutional.

Power Card 1: Legislative Branch

Congress can write bills, or proposals for new laws.

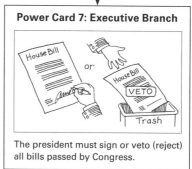

Power Card 7: Executive Branch

The president must sign or veto (reject) all bills passed by Congress.

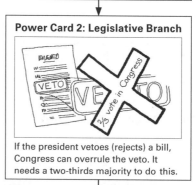

Power Card 2: Legislative Branch

If the president vetoes (rejects) a bill, Congress can overrule the veto. It needs a two-thirds majority to do this.

Power Card 14: Judicial Branch

The judicial branch can reject laws that are unconstitutional.

Chapter 14 Assessment

Big Ideas

Fill in the circle next to the best answer.

1. A weakness of the Articles of Confederation was that the central government
   - ○ A. was too strong.
   - ○ B. could not make war.
   - ○ C. could not pay its bills.
   - ○ D. took power from the states.

2. The men in Shays' Rebellion were fighting to
   - ○ A. free the slaves.
   - ○ B. unite the states.
   - ○ C. keep their homes.
   - ○ D. get out of the army.

3. Why did the states call a Constitutional Convention?
   - ○ A. to write state constitutions
   - ○ B. to organize political parties
   - ○ C. to break away from Great Britain
   - ○ D. to improve the Articles of Confederation

4. Which delegate from Virginia had a plan for a strong central government?
   - ○ A. James Madison
   - ○ B. Benjamin Franklin
   - ○ C. Gouverneur Morris
   - ○ D. George Washington

5. The Great Compromise was an agreement between
   - ○ A. rich and poor states.
   - ○ B. large and small states.
   - ○ C. northern and southern states.
   - ○ D. industrial and agricultural states.

6. Whose main job is to make laws?
   - ○ A. Congress
   - ○ B. governor
   - ○ C. president
   - ○ D. Supreme Court

7. The advisors to the head of the executive branch make up the
   - ○ A. ambassadors.
   - ○ B. cabinet.
   - ○ C. court.
   - ○ D. Senate.

8. After a government official is impeached, what happens next?
   - ○ A. The person goes to jail.
   - ○ B. The person must resign.
   - ○ C. The House holds a vote.
   - ○ D. The Senate holds a trial.

Reading Further

9. The judicial branch can decide whether a law is
   - ○ A. popular.
   - ○ B. reasonable.
   - ○ C. unconstitutional.
   - ○ D. wise.

10. Which term refers to the principle that nobody is above the law?
    - ○ A. rule of law
    - ○ B. limited powers
    - ○ C. checks and balances
    - ○ D. republican government

Social Studies Skills

Look at the drawing of the three-legged stool.
Find the crossbars A, B, and C.

The crossbars represent checks and balances.
Each connects two branches of government.
One branch limits the power of the other.

For each of the checks and balances below, decide
which two branches of government it involves.

- First, circle the letter of the crossbar connecting
  those two branches.

- Then, write a sentence explaining the connection.

The first one is completed for you.

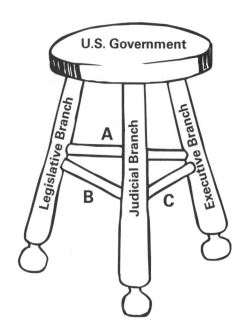

Example: Approve a treaty: (A) **B** **C**
After the president signs a treaty, the Senate must approve it.

11. Sign or veto a bill: **A** **B** **C**

12. Approve a cabinet member: **A** **B** **C**

13. Remove a judge for misuse of power: **A** **B** **C**

14. Pardon a person found guilty of a crime: **A** **B** **C**

Show You Know

15. Choose one of these four people. Circle the person's name.

James Madison   Gouverneur Morris

Benjamin Franklin   George Washington

Write a journal entry that person might have written during the Constitutional Convention. Your journal entry should include:

- the reason you are there
- your biggest hopes and fears
- one issue or point of discussion that concerns you
- how you see your personal role in the meeting
- a drawing to illustrate some part of the journal entry

Creating Living Scenes (Tableaux Vivants) for the Bill of Rights

Follow the steps below to create a living scene (tableau) that represents rights protected by the _____ Amendment. Your group will create a tableau that uses only your bodies and simple props. You will not speak during the presentation of the tableau.

Step 1: Brainstorm ideas for your tableau. Use your Reading Notes and your book to review information about your amendment. Then think about ideas for a tableau to represent the amendment.

Step 2: Collect or create simple props. Find or create simple props that you can use in your tableau to represent the rights protected by your amendment.

Step 3: Prepare to explain parts of your tableau. You will present your tableau to the class. Remember that you will pose silently during the presentation. Afterward, each group member will come to life, one at a time, and explain the part of the scene he or she represented. Each person in the group should practice explaining his or her part of the scene and get feedback from other group members.

Step 4: Practice presenting your tableau. Gather all your props and practice your poses for the tableau. Make sure that your group can clearly explain how your tableau represents the ideas in your amendment.

Chapter 15 Assessment

Big Ideas
Fill in the circle next to the best answer.

1. What is an amendment?
   ○ A. a resolution by the states
   ○ B. a law passed by Congress
   ○ C. a bill that guarantees a right
   ○ D. a change to the Constitution

2. After the Constitution was written, it had to be
   ○ A. reviewed by the court.
   ○ B. voted on by the people.
   ○ C. signed by the president.
   ○ D. ratified by nine of the states.

3. Which of these does the First Amendment protect?
   ○ A. printing lies about people
   ○ B. criticizing the government
   ○ C. making students pray in school
   ○ D. falsely shouting "fire" in a crowd

4. How did the Second Amendment explain the right to carry guns?
   ○ A. Big cities were dangerous.
   ○ B. The police were too strong.
   ○ C. States had volunteer armies.
   ○ D. People needed to fight duels.

5. Which amendment protects citizens against unreasonable search and seizure?
   ○ A. Fourth Amendment
   ○ B. Fifth Amendment
   ○ C. Sixth Amendment
   ○ D. Eighth Amendment

6. Which of these is an example of due process?
   ○ A. a fair trial
   ○ B. a prejudiced jury
   ○ C. a cruel punishment
   ○ D. a search without good reason

7. A civil trial would be most likely to result if Mary says that Ann
   ○ A. stole a car.
   ○ B. drove too fast.
   ○ C. owes her money.
   ○ D. set a fire in a school.

Reading Further
8. To appeal a court decision is to
   ○ A. organize a protest march.
   ○ B. request review by a higher court.
   ○ C. pay a fine instead of going to jail.
   ○ D. ask Congress to change a law.

Social Studies Skills

This illustration is about a real Supreme Court case in 1943 called *West Virginia Board of Education v. Barnette.* Use the illustration to answer the questions.

9. Which amendment was this court case about?

10. What did the school official want the student to do?

11. Explain the judge's decision in your own words.

12. Consider the judge's decision. When might a student not be allowed to use this form of free speech in school?

Show You Know

13. Suppose that you are living in the United States in April 1789. The country has a new Constitution but it does not yet have a Bill of Rights. Write a letter to a member of Congress. In your letter,

- explain why you think it is important to have a Bill of Rights.
- list one bad thing that happened in the colonies under British rule that shows the need for a Bill of Rights.
- list two specific rights you think the Bill of Rights should include.
- format your letter correctly.

Floor Map Labels

The United States in 1783

Atlantic Coastline of Original 13 Colonies

Louisiana Purchase (1803)

Florida Acquisition (1819)

Texas Annexation (1845)

Acquisition of Oregon Country (1846)

Mexican Cession (1848) and Gadsden Purchase (1853)

Experiencing Manifest Destiny

Acquisition 1: The United States in 1783

Step 1: Group 1 claims land along the Atlantic Coast on the floor map.

Step 2: Group 1 responds to these questions:
- Why did you settle where you did?
- Why do you think you are allowed to claim land only along the Atlantic Coast?

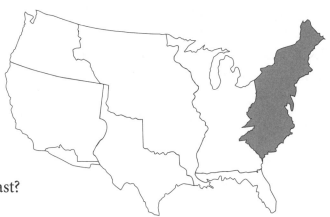

Step 3: All students read this background information: As a result of defeating the British in the American Revolution, the United States acquired new territory between the Appalachian Mountains and the Mississippi River. Some settlers who did not have land in the original 13 colonies soon moved into this region.

Step 4: Group 2 claims land in the remainder of the territory labeled "The United States in 1783."

Step 5: Group 2 responds to these questions:
- Why did you settle where you did?
- What do you think should be done with the territories west of where you have settled?

Acquisition 2: Louisiana Purchase (1803)

Step 1: All students read this background information:
In 1803, President Thomas Jefferson purchased the Louisiana Territory from the French leader, Napoleon. The area, which was purchased for $15 million, extended roughly from the Mississippi River to the Rocky Mountains. The Louisiana Purchase more than doubled the size of the United States.

Step 2: The student representing President Thomas Jefferson prepares a check for France for the purchase of the Louisiana Territory.

Step 3: Group 3 claims land in the Louisiana Purchase.

Step 4: Group 3 responds to these questions:
- Why did you settle where you did?
- What do you think should be done with the territories west of where you have settled?

Acquisition 3: Florida Acquisition (1819)

Step 1: All students read this background information:
During the early 1800s, American settlements in Georgia were often raided by American Indians. Frustrated, the settlers blamed Spanish officials in Florida for encouraging these attacks. In addition, Georgia's settlers were upset that Florida was becoming a safe place for runaway slaves. Many Americans expected President James Monroe to resolve these problems.

Step 2: Groups 1, 2, and 3 decide what the United States should do:
A. Have U.S. troops defend the border between Georgia and Florida.
B. Send U.S. troops into Florida to pursue the Seminoles.
C. Negotiate with the Spanish to see if they will sell Florida to the United States.

Step 3: All students read about what the United States actually did:
In 1817, U.S. General Andrew Jackson marched to Florida to end Seminole raids. He then attacked the Spanish capital at Pensacola. As a result, in 1819, the Spanish agreed to give up their claim to Florida. In exchange, the United States agreed to pay $5 million in claims that settlers had made against Spain for those Seminole border raids.

Step 4: The student representing President James Monroe prepares a check for Georgia's settlers. This will compensate them for their losses during border raids.

Step 5: Group 4 claims land in the Florida territory.

Step 6: Group 4 responds to these questions:
- Why did you settle where you did?
- What do you think should be done with the territories west of where you have settled?

Acquisition 4: Texas Annexation (1845)

Step 1: All students read this background information:
During the 1820s, many Americans began moving into Texas. At the time, Texas was controlled by Mexico. In 1836, however, Texas won its independence in a war with Mexico. Many Americans and Texans thought that the United States should annex Texas—that is, make the territory part of the United States. Others worried that such a move would hurt relations between the United States and Mexico. In 1845, President John Tyler decided he must act.

Step 2: Groups 1, 2, 3, and 4 decide what the United States should do:
A. Ask Congress to approve annexing Texas.
B. Help Mexico regain control of Texas.
C. Ignore the request to make Texas part of the United States.

Step 3: All students read about what the United States actually did:
In response to popular support for annexing Texas, President Tyler called for Congress to vote on the matter. Congress quickly approved a proposal to invite Texas to become part of the United States. Several months later, Texans voted to join the United States. The Lone Star Republic became a new state shortly thereafter.

Step 4: Group 5 claims land in Texas.

Step 5: Group 5 responds to these questions:
- Why did you settle where you did?
- What do you think should be done with the territories west of where you have settled?

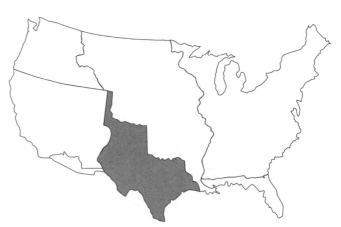

Acquisition 5: Acquisition of Oregon Country (1846)

Step 1: All students read this background information:
In 1845, a disagreement developed between the United States and Great Britain over who controlled Oregon Country. Settlers from both Great Britain and the United States were living in Oregon, but most of the settlers were American. Americans pressured their new president, James K. Polk, to annex Oregon Country, just as the United States had done with Texas.

Step 2: Groups 1, 2, 3, 4, and 5 decide what the United States should do:
A. Send soldiers to Oregon Country so that the territory can be annexed.
B. Divide Oregon Country between Great Britain and the United States.
C. Sell Oregon Country to the British for $15 million.

Step 3: All students read about what the United States actually did:
Despite pressure from many Americans to take control of all of Oregon Country, President Polk offered to divide the territory between the United States and Britain. In a treaty signed in 1846, the two countries agreed that the 49th parallel would be the boundary between British Canada and the United States west of the Rocky Mountains.

Step 4: Group 6 claims land in Oregon Country.

Step 5: Group 6 responds to these questions:
- Why did you settle where you did?
- What do you think should be done with the territories south of where you have settled?

Acquisition 6: Mexican Cession (1848) and Gadsden Purchase (1853)

Step 1: All students read this background information:
Once Texas gained its independence from Mexico in 1836, there was an ongoing conflict between the two countries about the location of the southern boundary of Texas. Mexico insisted that the border was at the Nueces River. Texans insisted that the border was about 150 miles to the south, along the Rio Grande. Once again, many Americans expected President Polk to promote the expansion of the United States.

Step 2: All groups decide what the United States should do:
A. Negotiate with Mexico to establish a new southern border for Texas.

B. Offer to buy from Mexico the area between the Nueces River and the Rio Grande.

C. Send troops into Texas to maintain the border along the Rio Grande.

Step 3: All students read about what the United States actually did:
In 1846, President Polk sent troops to the Rio Grande. Soon, war broke out between the two countries. After two years of fighting, the United States captured Mexico City and won the war. In the peace treaty, Mexico recognized the Rio Grande as the southern border of Texas and gave the United States the Mexican Cession. In return, the United States paid Mexico $15 million. Five years later, the United States paid Mexico $10 million for the Gadsden Purchase.

Step 4: Four students—representing casualties in the war with Mexico—walk off the floor map and return to their seats.

Step 5: The student representing President James Polk prepares two checks for Mexico. These will pay for the land in the Mexican Cession and the Gadsden Purchase.

Step 6: All groups claim land in the territory acquired by both the Mexican Cession and the Gadsden Purchase.

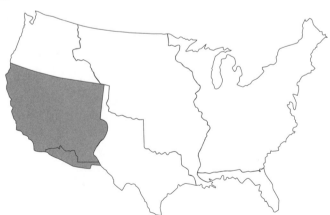

© Teachers' Curriculum Institute

Blank Checks

Date _____ **10_**

Pay to the
order of _____ $ [   ]

_____ *Dollars*

Bank of the
United States

For _____   _____
                                        AUTHORIZED SIGNATURE

II⁰ 0004162071   0111200365   93860 157486   II⁰

Date _____ **10_**

Pay to the
order of _____ $ [   ]

_____ *Dollars*

Bank of the
United States

For _____   _____
                                        AUTHORIZED SIGNATURE

II⁰ 0004162071   0111200365   93860 157486   II⁰

Chapter 16 Assessment

Big Ideas

Fill in the circle next to the best answer.

1. Why did the United States want new acquisitions in the West?
   ○ A. to have closer ties with Europe
   ○ B. to protect the natural environment
   ○ C. to study American Indian cultures
   ○ D. to give people from the United States more land to farm and live on

2. Manifest destiny was the belief that the United States should
   ○ A. expand to the Pacific Ocean.
   ○ B. honor claims by other countries.
   ○ C. give all citizens the right to vote.
   ○ D. treat native peoples with respect.

3. Jefferson agreed to buy French land to the west so that
   ○ A. runaway slaves could not hide there.
   ○ B. American Indians would have a place to live.
   ○ C. American goods could move through New Orleans.
   ○ D. the United States would have an ally against Great Britain.

4. The United States got Florida from
   ○ A. France.
   ○ B. Great Britain.
   ○ C. Mexico.
   ○ D. Spain.

5. Many Americans in Texas wanted freedom from Mexico so they could
   ○ A. get free land.
   ○ B. keep their slaves.
   ○ C. build homes at the Alamo.
   ○ D. help the American Indians.

6. The United States and Great Britain agreed on a boundary for the
   ○ A. Oregon Country.
   ○ B. Mexican Cession.
   ○ C. Gadsden Purchase.
   ○ D. Louisiana Purchase.

7. Why did Mexico give up the territory called the Mexican Cession?
   ○ A. It received a large price.
   ○ B. It traded for other territory.
   ○ C. It had just lost a fierce war.
   ○ D. It did not want desert lands.

8. What was the main reason American Indians went onto reservations?
   ○ A. They wanted better farmland.
   ○ B. The U.S. government forced them to move.
   ○ C. Buffalo herds led them there.
   ○ D. They formed an alliance with Mexicans.

Social Studies Skills

Use the map and timeline to answer the questions. Write your answers below.

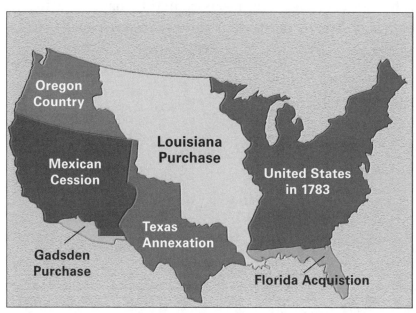

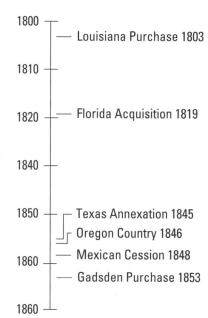

9. Add these two events at the appropriate places on the timeline:
   a. Lewis and Clark Expedition, 1804–1806
   b. Texas independence, 1836

10. The route of the Lewis and Clark Expedition passed through the areas of two territorial acquisitions shown on the map.
   a. Which of those areas already belonged to the United States when the expedition traveled there? _____
   b. Which of those areas did not yet belong to the United States? _____
   c. How many years after the end of the expedition did the United States acquire the area you named above? _____

11. For how many years was Texas an independent republic? _____

12. In which year did the United States buy the smallest of the territorial acquisitions shown on the map? _____

Reading Further

13. How long after the Louisiana Purchase was the Cherokee Trail of Tears (1838)?

   _____

14. Find the area where the Trail of Tears began. How is that area labeled on the map?

Show You Know

15. Suppose that you are a newspaper editor in the eastern United States in the 1800s. You have gone to one of the territorial acquisitions discussed in this chapter, during the time it came under U.S. control. Write a brief editorial for your newspaper. Include these items:

- the name and date of the territory or acquisition
- why the United States wanted that territory
- how the United States got that territory
- a quotation from somebody you interviewed, such as a settler, a soldier, a Mexican, or an American Indian
- an opinion about whether you think this acquisition is good for the United States, and why or why not
- a picture to go with your article (newspaper pictures in the 1800s were drawings)

Preparing an Interactive Dramatization: Mexicanos

Work with your group to create an interactive dramatization about Mexicanos. Follow the steps below.

____ **Step 1: Review the roles**. After your teacher assigns your role, read the information below. Make sure that everyone understands his or her responsibilities.

Historian: You will lead the group during Step 2. Make sure that everyone understands and uses key historical information about Mexicanos.
Director: You will lead the group during Step 3. Make sure that everyone is equally involved and that the dramatization includes all the required elements.

Set Designer: You will lead the group during Step 4 as it organizes and gathers costumes and props. You are responsible for making sure that the dramatization is as realistic as possible.

Host: You will lead the group during Step 5 as it rehearses its dramatization. During the presentation, you will invite audience members to participate, and then you will answer any questions they have.

____ **Step 2: Learn about Mexicanos.** Carefully examine your placard to see what the image reveals about Mexicanos. Then take turns reading aloud the information about Mexicanos in Section 17.3 of your book. When you finish reading, the Historian should record the group's answers to these questions:

1. How did the Mexican government encourage wealthy Mexicanos to settle in California in the early 1800s?

2. Who were vaqueros, and what important pieces of equipment did they use?

3. What are two important ways in which Mexicanos adapted to the environment of the West?

4. How were Mexicanos treated when the West became part of the United States in 1848?

____ **Step 3: Create your dramatization.** You must present a three- to five-minute interactive dramatization about Mexicanos that involves each group member and four members of the audience. You may use the song "La Discriminación" from CD Track 3 during your presentation. Your teacher will give you the words to the song. Your dramatization must make audience members feel as if they are observing a group of Mexicanos on a rancho. The Director should make sure that everyone has a role and that the dramatization includes the following parts, in this order:

1. Greet your visitors with the Spanish term *buenos dias* (BUAY-nohs DEE-ahs), which means "hello."

2. Say, "We have created successful settlements in the dry environment of the Southwest. Anglos (English-speaking Americans) can learn a great deal from us," and explain what you mean.

3. Have your visitors walk out to an orchard that is being irrigated. Have them dig part of an irrigation channel, and explain to them why irrigation is so important in the West. Tell your visitors that Mexicanos have been using irrigation in this dry land for hundreds of years.

4. Tell your visitors to pick some oranges off one of the trees in the orchard. Point out other crops that are growing on the rancho, such as lemons and grapes. Explain that these crops first came from Spain, which also has a dry climate.

5. Have your visitors put on *sombreros* and *chaparreras,* and explain why vaqueros wear this clothing. Then have the visitors mount horses, and show them how to rope cattle with a *reata*.

6. When you return from your horseback ride, point to some of the *adobe* buildings on the rancho. Explain how the buildings are made from adobe bricks. Have your visitors pour some mud into a wooden mold.

7. Take your visitors inside the rancho's kitchen. Offer them warm *tortillas* and *carne asada*.

____ **Step 4: Brainstorm ideas for costumes and props.** Your dramatization must be as realistic as possible. Before you begin creating costumes and props, the Set Designer—using ideas from the group—should complete the checklists below.

List Costumes you will include in your dramatization	List materials needed to create costumes	Identify group member(s) responsible for creating costumes
List props you will include in your dramatization	**List materials needed to create props**	**Identify group member(s) responsible for creating props**

____ **Step 5: Rehearse your dramatization.** After you have created costumes and props, make sure that you can present your dramatization in three to five minutes. As you rehearse, the Host should make sure that
- each group member is actively involved in the dramatization.
- the dramatization flows smoothly.
- a cue has been created to signal when the Director should play the song.
- costumes and props are used effectively.
- lines are spoken at an appropriate volume.
- four members of the audience have been identified to participate in the dramatization.

Preparing an Interactive Dramatization: Forty-Niners

Work with your group to create an interactive dramatization about forty-niners. Follow the steps below.

_____ **Step 1: Review the roles.** After your teacher assigns your role, read the information below. Make sure that everyone understands his or her responsibilities.

Historian: You will lead the group during Step 2. Make sure that everyone understands and uses key historical information about forty-niners.

Director: You will lead the group during Step 3. Make sure that everyone is equally involved and that the dramatization includes all the required elements.

Set Designer: You will lead the group during Step 4 as it organizes and gathers costumes and props. You are responsible for making sure that the dramatization is as realistic as possible.

Host: You will lead the group during Step 5 as it rehearses its dramatization. During the presentation, you will invite audience members to participate, and then you will answer any questions they have.

_____ **Step 2: Learn about forty-niners.** Carefully examine your placard to see what the image reveals about forty-niners. Then take turns reading aloud the information about forty-niners in Section 17.4 of your book. When you finish reading, the Historian should record the group's answers to these questions:

1. What brought forty-niners to the West in the 1800s?

2. How did forty-niners do their jobs?

3. Describe the mining camps of forty-niners.

4. What did most forty-niners do after failing to find large quantities of gold in California?

____ Step 3: Create your dramatization. You must present a three- to five-minute interactive dramatization about forty-niners that involves each group member and four members of the audience. You may use the sound effects from CD Track 4 during your presentation. Your dramatization must make audience members feel as if they are observing a group of forty-niners prospecting for gold. The Director should make sure that everyone has a role and that the dramatization includes the following parts, in this order:

1. Greet your visitors. Encourage them to stand around the sluice you are using to separate gold from gravel.

2. Introduce yourselves. Explain that you are working a claim in a goldfield.

3. Have your visitors shovel some gravel into the steady stream of water that flows through the sluice. Point out how gold and other heavy particles sink to the bottom.

4. One of you—representing an African American miner—should show a drawing of family members, who live in the South. Explain how you plan to use your mining profits to free your relatives from slavery and move them to California.

5. Offer your visitors some sourdough bread.

6. Explain how you think that many local store owners take advantage of miners.

7. Ask your visitors if they know of any women who would like to move to California. Explain how nearly all forty-niners are looking for wives.

8. Say, "It's amazing how well we get along without any courts or law," and explain what you mean.

_____ **Step 4: Brainstorm ideas for costumes and props.** Your dramatization must be as realistic as possible. Before you begin creating costumes and props, the Set Designer—using ideas from the group—should complete the checklists below.

List Costumes you will include in your dramatization	List materials needed to create costumes	Identify group member(s) responsible for creating costumes
List props you will include in your dramatization	List materials needed to create props	Identify group member(s) responsible for creating props

_____ **Step 5: Rehearse your dramatization.** After you have created costumes and props, make sure that you can present your dramatization in three to five minutes. As you rehearse, the Host should make sure that

• each group member is actively involved in the dramatization.

• the dramatization flows smoothly.

• a cue has been created to signal when the Director should play the sound effects.

• costumes and props are used effectively.

• lines are spoken at an appropriate volume.

• four members of the audience have been identified to participate in the dramatization.

Preparing an Interactive Dramatization: Chinese Immigrants

Work with your group to create an interactive dramatization about Chinese immigrants. Follow the steps below.

_____ **Step 1: Review the roles.** After your teacher assigns your role, read the information below. Make sure that everyone understands his or her responsibilities.

Historian: You will lead the group during Step 2. Make sure that everyone understands and uses key historical information about Chinese immigrants.

Director: You will lead the group during Step 3. Make sure that everyone is equally involved and that the dramatization includes all the required elements.

Set Designer: You will lead the group during Step 4 as it organizes and gathers costumes, props, and scenery. You are responsible for making sure that the dramatization is as realistic as possible.

Host: You will lead the group during Step 5 as it rehearses its dramatization. During the presentation, you will invite audience members to participate, and then you will answer any questions they have.

_____ **Step 2: Learn about Chinese immigrants.** Carefully examine your placard to see what the image reveals about Chinese immigrants. Then take turns reading aloud the information about Chinese immigrants in Section 17.5 of your book. When you finish reading, the Historian should record the group's answers to these questions:

1. Why did Chinese immigrants settle in the West in the 1800s?

2. How did Chinese immigrants help build the transcontinental railroad?

3. How was life difficult for Chinese immigrants?.

4. What was the Chinese Exclusion Act? Why was it passed?

____ **Step 3: Create your dramatization.** You must present a three- to five-minute interactive dramatization about Chinese immigrants that involves each group member and four members of the audience. You can use the sound effects from CD Track 5 during your presentation. Your dramatization must make audience members feel as if they are observing a group of Chinese immigrants digging a tunnel for the transcontinental railroad. The Director should make sure that everyone has a role and that the dramatization includes the following parts, in this order:

1. Greet your visitors. Show them the wicker basket, gunpowder, and matches that you are using to build a tunnel in the side of a mountain.

2. Explain how you will dig holes in the mountain and insert gunpowder and fuses to blow a hole through the rock.

3. Have your visitors help raise one of you up the side of the mountain in the wicker basket.

4. Point to a grave at the base of the mountain. Explain how one of your friends died while helping to build the transcontinental railroad.

5. Have your visitors examine the gold coins you were awarded by a railroad boss. Explain that you received the coins after winning a track-laying contest.

6. Show your visitors the wound you received while fighting a war in China. Explain why the war forced you to leave your homeland.

7. Bring your visitors to your camp. Show them the letters you are writing to your families, who are still living in China.

8. Say, "The Chinese Exclusion Act is unfair," and explain what you mean.

_____ **Step 4: Brainstorm ideas for costumes and props.** Your dramatization must be as realistic as possible. Before you begin creating costumes and props, the Set Designer—using ideas from the group—should complete the checklists below.

List Costumes you will include in your dramatization	List materials needed to create costumes	Identify group member(s) responsible for creating costumes
List props you will include in your dramatization	List materials needed to create props	Identify group member(s) responsible for creating props

_____ **Step 5: Rehearse your dramatization.** After you have created costumes and props, make sure that you can present your dramatization in three to five minutes. As you rehearse, the Host should make sure that

- each group member is actively involved in the dramatization.
- the dramatization flows smoothly.
- a cue has been created to signal when the Director should play the sound effects.
- costumes and props are used effectively.
- lines are spoken at an appropriate volume.
- four members of the audience have been identified to participate in the dramatization.

Preparing an Interactive Dramatization: Mormons

Work with your group to create an interactive dramatization about Mormon settlers. Follow the steps below.

_____ **Step 1: Review the roles.** After your teacher assigns your role, read the information below. Make sure that everyone understands his or her responsibilities.

Historian: You will lead the group during Step 2. Make sure that everyone understands and uses key historical information about Mormon settlers.

Director: You will lead the group during Step 3. Make sure that everyone is equally involved and that the dramatization includes all the required elements.

Set Designer: You will lead the group during Step 4 as it organizes and gathers costumes and props. You are responsible for making sure that the dramatization is as realistic as possible.

Host: You will lead the group during Step 5 as it rehearses its dramatization. During the presentation, you will invite audience members to participate, and then you will answer any questions they have.

_____ **Step 2: Learn about Mormon settlers.** Carefully examine your placard to see what the image reveals about Mormon settlers. Then take turns reading aloud the information about the Mormons in Section 17.6 of your book. When you finish reading, the Historian should record the group's answers to these questions:

1. Who founded the Mormon Church? What were his key teachings?

2. Why did the Mormons have to move from place to place before settling in Utah?

3. Who was Brigham Young? How did he help the Mormons?

4. What did the Mormons do to make sure that they would never be forced out of Utah?

____ **Step 3: Create your dramatization.** You must present a three-to five-minute interactive dramatization about Mormon settlers that involves each group member and four members of the audience. You can use the sound effects from CD Track 6 during your presentation. Your dramatization must make audience members feel as if they are observing a group of Mormons moving along the trail to Utah. The Director should make sure that everyone has a role and that the dramatization includes the following parts, in this order:

1. Greet your visitors and introduce the people in your group.

2. Unfold a map and show your visitors that you are traveling from Illinois to Utah.

3. Point to the states of Ohio and Illinois on the map. Explain why Mormons had to leave those states.

4. Explain to your visitors how Joseph Smith was murdered after he established the Mormon Church.

5. Show your visitors the tools and supplies in your wagon. Explain what Brigham Young did to make sure that Mormons reached Utah safely.

6. Have your visitors examine a buffalo skull at the side of the road. Explain how you use these skulls to communicate with other Mormons making the journey to Utah.

7. Point to the handcart in the image in your book or one you have made. Explain how poor European Mormons use these—with no help from mules or oxen—to carry their possessions along the trail to Utah.

8. Say, "We are willing to set aside our personal goals and work for the good of the Mormon community," and explain what you mean.

____ Step 4: Brainstorm ideas for costumes and props. Your dramatization must be as realistic as possible. Before you begin creating costumes and props, the Set Designer—using ideas from the group—should complete the checklists below.

List Costumes you will include in your dramatization	List materials needed to create costumes	Identify group member(s) responsible for creating costumes
List props you will include in your dramatization	List materials needed to create props	Identify group member(s) responsible for creating props

____ Step 5: Rehearse your dramatization. After you have created costumes and props, make sure that you can present your dramatization in three to five minutes. As you rehearse, the Host should make sure that

- each group member is actively involved in the dramatization.

- the dramatization flows smoothly.

- a cue has been created to signal when the Director should play the sound effects.

- costumes and props are used effectively.

- lines are spoken at an appropriate volume.

- four members of the audience have been identified to participate in the dramatization.

Preparing an Interactive Dramatization: Oregon Pioneers

Work with your group to create an interactive dramatization about Oregon pioneers. Follow the steps below.

_____ **Step 1: Review the roles.** After your teacher assigns your role, read the information below. Make sure that everyone understands his or her responsibilities.

Historian: You will lead the group during Step 2. Make sure that everyone understands and uses key historical information about Oregon pioneers.

Director: You will lead the group during Step 3. Make sure that everyone is equally involved and that the dramatization includes all the required elements.

Set Designer: You will lead the group during Step 4 as it organizes and gathers costumes, props, and scenery. You are responsible for making sure that the dramatization is as realistic as possible.

Host: You will lead the group during Step 5 as it rehearses its dramatization. During the presentation, you will invite audience members to participate, and then you will answer any questions they have.

_____ **Step 2: Learn about Oregon pioneers.** Carefully examine your placard to see what the image reveals about Oregon pioneers. Then take turns reading aloud the information about Oregon pioneers in Section 17.7 of your book. When you finish reading, the Historian should record the group's answers to these questions:

1. How did people learn about Oregon Country in the 1800s?

2. What types of supplies did pioneers usually bring on the trip to Oregon?

3. How was life difficult for pioneers along the Oregon Trail?

4. How did American Indians treat pioneers moving along the Oregon Trail?

____ **Step 3: Create your dramatization.** You must present a three-to five-minute interactive dramatization about Oregon pioneers that involves each group member and four members of the audience. You may use the sound effects from CD Track 7 during your presentation. Your dramatization must make audience members feel as if they are observing a pioneer family making their way to Oregon. The Director should make sure that everyone has a role and that the dramatization includes the following parts, in this order:

1. Greet your visitors and explain why you are moving to Oregon.

2. Take your visitors to the back of your wagon. Have them give a cup of water to the sick children lying inside.

3. Describe how life is difficult along the Oregon Trail.

4. Have your visitors examine a few of the supplies that are packed in your wagon, such as cookware and tools. Explain why these items are important to you.

5. One of you, acting as a pioneer woman, should show your visitors your diary. Read an entry to your visitors that describes the demanding work that women do each day.

6. Have your visitors help you remove the yoke from your oxen.

7. Say, "While the journey to Oregon is difficult, our lives will be better once we get there," and explain what you mean.

_____ **Step 4: Brainstorm ideas for costumes and props.** Your dramatization must be as realistic as possible. Before you begin creating costumes and props, the Set Designer—using ideas from the group—should complete the checklists below.

List Costumes you will include in your dramatization	List materials needed to create costumes	Identify group member(s) responsible for creating costumes
List props you will include in your dramatization	List materials needed to create props	Identify group member(s) responsible for creating props

_____ **Step 5: Rehearse your dramatization.** After you have created costumes and props, make sure that you can present your dramatization in three to five minutes. As you rehearse, the Host should make sure that

- each group member is actively involved in the dramatization.
- the dramatization flows smoothly.
- a cue has been created to signal when the Director should play the sound effects.
- costumes and props are used effectively.
- lines are spoken at an appropriate volume.
- four members of the audience have been identified to participate in the dramatization.

Preparing an Interactive Dramatization: Nez Percés

Work with your group to create an interactive dramatization about the Nez Percés. Follow the steps below.

_____ **Step 1: Review the roles**. After your teacher assigns your role, read the information below. Make sure that everyone understands his or her responsibilities.

Historian: You will lead the group during Step 2. Make sure that everyone understands and uses key historical information about the Nez Percés.

Director: You will lead the group during Step 3. Make sure that everyone is equally involved and that the dramatization includes all the required elements.

Set Designer: You will lead the group during Step 4 as it organizes and gathers costumes and props. You are responsible for making sure that the dramatization is as realistic as possible.

Host: You will lead the group during Step 5 as it rehearses its dramatization. During the presentation, you will invite audience members to participate, and then you will answer any questions they have.

_____ **Step 2: Learn about the Nez Percés**. Carefully examine your placard to see what the image reveals about the Nez Percés. Then take turns reading aloud the information about the Nez Percés in Section 17.8 of your book. When you finish reading, the Historian should record the group's answers to these questions:

1. Where did the Nez Percés live? Describe their way of life.

2. How did the arrival of white settlers change the lives of the Nez Percés?

3. Why did Chief Joseph lead the Nez Percés north toward Canada?

4. What happened to the Nez Percés after Chief Joseph surrendered to the U.S. Army?

____ **Step 3: Create your dramatization.** You must present a three- to five-minute interactive dramatization about the Nez Percés that involves each group member and four members of the audience. You may use the sound effects from CD Track 8 during your presentation. Your dramatization must make audience members feel as if they are observing a group of Nez Percés on a reservation in Oklahoma. The Director should make sure that everyone has a role and that the dramatization includes the following parts, in this order:

1. Introduce yourselves and explain that you are Nez Percés who have been forced to live on this reservation in Oklahoma.

2. Give your visitors a quick tour of the reservation. Point out the number of Nez Percés who are dying of sickness and starvation.

3. Unfold a copy of a treaty stating that the U.S. government reserves land in the Wallowa Valley for the Nez Percés. Explain how the government failed to keep its promise.

4. Draw a map on the ground to explain how the Nez Percés were driven from their homes in the Wallowa Valley to the Canadian border, and finally to Oklahoma.

5. Show your visitors a rock with blood on it. Tell them that the blood is from your daughter, and explain how she died in the Bear Paw Mountains.

6. Read the following lines from Chief Joseph's speech as he surrendered to the U.S. Army: "Hear me, my chiefs. I am tired; my heart is sick and sad. From where the sun now stands, I will fight no more, forever."

7. Ask your visitors how Chief Joseph's speech makes them feel. Explain why the speech is important to the Nez Percés.

8. Ask your visitors to write a letter to the U.S. government explaining that the Nez Percés have been treated unjustly.

_____ **Step 4: Brainstorm ideas for costumes and props.** Your dramatization must be as realistic as possible. Before you begin creating costumes and props, the Set Designer—using ideas from the group—should complete the checklists below.

List Costumes you will include in your dramatization	List materials needed to create costumes	Identify group member(s) responsible for creating costumes
List props you will include in your dramatization	List materials needed to create props	Identify group member(s) responsible for creating props

_____ **Step 5: Rehearse your dramatization.** After you have created costumes and props, make sure that you can present your dramatization in three to five minutes. As you rehearse, the Host should make sure that

- each group member is actively involved in the dramatization.

- the dramatization flows smoothly.

- a cue has been created to signal when the Director should play the sound effects.

- costumes and props are used effectively.

- lines are spoken at an appropriate volume.

- four members of the audience have been identified to participate in the dramatization.

"La Discriminación"

Spanish	English
La Discriminación	**Discrimination**

La Discriminación

Con tristeza y sin remedo
voy a decir lo que siento
y sin referirme a nadie

para no hacer argumento
solo culpo mi destino
con profundo sentimiento.

No más tan solo en pensar
en las discriminaciónes
que sufrimos los Latinos
en ranchos y poblaciónes
nos distinguen como ovejas
algunos anglosajones.

No me refiero a nadie
para no hacer argumento,
pertenezco a Estados Unidos
de seguro cien por ciento,
nadie me quita el derecho
pero guardo un sentimiento.

Yo nací en el estado de Tejas
y he crecido con afanes,
trabajando por la vida
y enriqueciendo por la vida
he sufrido los desprecios
de tejanos alemanes.

No me duele lo que soy
como el caso de Longoria*
en el estado de Tejas.

En mi despedida ruego
que me otorguen el perdón
que en lo que digo no miento
no me distingo nación
que en todas los continentes
hay la discriminación.

Discrimination

It is with sadness and hopelessness
that I'm going to say what I feel,
I won't mention any names

so there won't be any arguments,
I can only blame my destiny
with a profound sense of grief.

Just to think about
the discrimination
that we Latinos suffer
in the fields and towns,
we are looked upon as sheep
by some Anglo-Saxons.

I won't mention any names
so there won't be any arguments,
I belong to the United States
without a doubt, a hundred percent,
no one can take away that right
but nevertheless, I carry a grudge.

I was born in the state of Texas
and growing up has been a struggle
while working to survive
I have enriched scoundrels,
I have suffered the disdain
of German Texans.

I don't feel sorry about myself
like the Longoria case*
in the state of Texas.

I hope in this my farewell
that you will excuse me
but what I say is true;
I won't single out any nation
since in all the continents
there is discrimination.

*Felix Longoria, a decorated World War II hero, was refused burial by a funeral agency in his hometown in South Texas. His wife believed that this happened because he was a Mexican American, but the owners of the funeral home denied that this was the reason.

Chapter 17 Assessment

Big Ideas
Fill in the circle next to the best answer.

1. Some newcomers to the West learned the skills to be cowboys from the
   - ○ A. Mexicanos.
   - ○ B. Mormons.
   - ○ C. Nez Percés.
   - ○ D. pioneers.

2. Why did the owners of many ranchos in the United States speak Spanish?
   - ○ A. Rich families moved to America from Spain.
   - ○ B. The United States acquired the land from Mexico.
   - ○ C. Settlers from the East Coast learned how to speak Spanish.
   - ○ D. Immigrants came from Latin America to seek a better life.

3. The forty-niners traveled west for
   - ○ A. gold.
   - ○ B. free land.
   - ○ C. railroad jobs.
   - ○ D. religious freedom.

4. What was a miner's claim?
   - ○ A. the food the miner ate
   - ○ B. the tools the miner used
   - ○ C. the land the miner worked
   - ○ D. the money the miner saved

5. Many Chinese immigrants found work helping to build
   - ○ A. Salt Lake City.
   - ○ B. the Oregon Trail.
   - ○ C. San Francisco Harbor.
   - ○ D. the transcontinental railroad.

6. Which state was settled mainly by Mormons?
   - ○ A. California
   - ○ B. Oregon
   - ○ C. Texas
   - ○ D. Utah

7. Why did Chief Joseph lead the Nez Percés toward Canada?
   - ○ A. to settle on a reservation
   - ○ B. to be safe from U.S. soldiers
   - ○ C. to find rivers with more salmon
   - ○ D. to start a war against the settlers

Reading Further
8. How did the Homestead Act encourage people to move west?
   - ○ A. It paid money for their old homes.
   - ○ B. It made peace with the American Indians.
   - ○ C. It offered settlers cheap or free land.
   - ○ D. It filled eastern cities with immigrants.

Social Studies Skills

Amelia Stewart Knight kept a diary about moving to the Oregon Territory from Iowa in 1853. Read these parts from her diary about the Oregon Trail. Answer the questions below.

Thursday, April 14th – We have traveled 24 miles today and are about to camp in a large prairie without wood. The men . . . are hunting something to make a fire to get supper.

Friday, April 15th – Bad luck last night. Three of our horses got away. Roads very bad and muddy.

Thursday, April 21st – I have just counted 17 wagons traveling ahead of us in the mud and water. No feed for our poor stock . . . Have to feed them flour and meal.

Saturday, April 23rd – Still in camp, it rained hard all night, and blew a hurricane almost. All the tents were blown down, and some wagons capsized. One of the oxen missing; . . . crowded in the tent, cold and wet and uncomfortable in the wagon. No place for the poor children. I have been busy cooking . . .

Tuesday, August 2nd – Traveled 12 miles today and have just camped about one-half mile from the river. Plenty of good grass.

Wednesday, August 17th – Bought some fresh salmon from the Indians this evening, which is quite a treat to us. It is the first we have seen.

Saturday, September 17th – We picked up and ferried across the Columbia River, using skiff, canoes and flatboat to get across, taking three days to complete. Here husband traded two yoke [pair] of oxen for a half section of land with one-half acre planted to potatoes and a small log cabin and lean-to with no windows.

---

9. Describe three hardships Knight's family experienced on the trail.

10. According to the diary, why was the lack of wood on the prairie a problem?

11. Why do you think Knight mentioned having grass at one campsite?

12. What does the diary show about relations with the American Indians?

13. How did Knight's family cross the Columbia River?

14. Describe the family's first home in Oregon and how they got it.

Show You Know

15. On a separate piece of paper, create a billboard that advertises the factors that encouraged groups to move to the West. Make sure your billboard includes these:

    • at least three simple drawings or visual symbols that represent different reasons why the groups you studied moved to the West.

    • a short, catchy slogan that summarizes the reasons why groups moved to the West.

    • graffiti along the bottom of the billboard that represents how a member of one of the groups that did not benefit from the settlement of the West might feel about the ideas represented on the billboard. Use appropriate language and drawings for the graffiti.

Chapter 18 Assessment

Big Ideas
Fill in the circle next to the best answer.

1. Compared with the North, the South had more
   - ○ A. cities.
   - ○ B. factories.
   - ○ C. plantations.
   - ○ D. railroads.

2. Why were workers in the North called "free labor"?
   - ○ A. They worked for no money.
   - ○ B. They came from other countries.
   - ○ C. They usually did not have families.
   - ○ D. They could choose their own jobs.

3. What was the most important crop in the South by the mid-1800s?
   - ○ A. corn
   - ○ B. cotton
   - ○ C. rice
   - ○ D. tobacco

4. What was a goal of the Missouri Compromise?
   - ○ A. returning fugitive slaves
   - ○ B. preventing slavery in the cities
   - ○ C. keeping an equal number of slave states and free states
   - ○ D. letting each territory decide whether to allow slavery

5. People like Frederick Douglas who spoke out against slavery were called
   - ○ A. abolitionists.
   - ○ B. slave owners.
   - ○ C. enslaved African Americans.
   - ○ D. conductors on the Underground Railroad.

6. Which statement is true of the Compromise of 1850?
   - ○ A. Abraham Lincoln proposed the new law.
   - ○ B. Most Americans were happy with the results.
   - ○ C. Officials no longer had to return fugitive slaves.
   - ○ D. California was admitted to the Union as a free state.

7. Kansas was called "Bleeding Kansas" in the 1850s because of
   - ○ A. violent fights about slavery.
   - ○ B. attacks by American Indians.
   - ○ C. deadly diseases among settlers.
   - ○ D. injuries from putting up fences.

8. Which group was most angry about the election of Abraham Lincoln?
   - ○ A. enslaved Africans
   - ○ B. Southern slave owners
   - ○ C. Northern factory owners
   - ○ D. German and Irish immigrants

Reading Further
9. *Uncle Tom's Cabin* was most important because it promoted
   - ○ A. construction of canals.
   - ○ B. settlement of the West.
   - ○ C. manufacture of weapons.
   - ○ D. opinion against slavery.

Social Studies Skills

Use the map to answer the questions. Write your answer on the line provided.

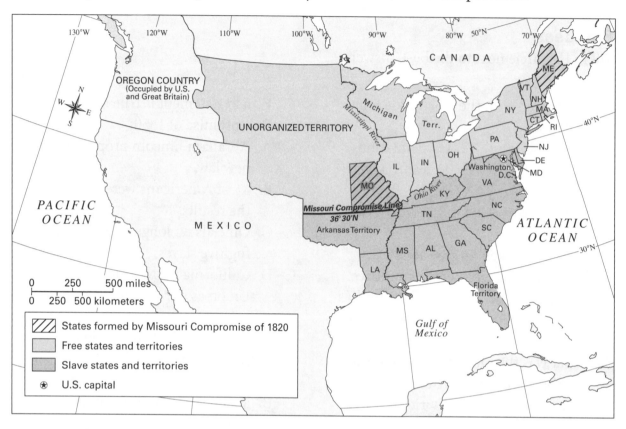

10. Name three territories shown on the map (not counting "unorganized territory").
    Beside each one, circle "S" if slavery was allowed there, and "F" if it was not allowed.

    a. _____ S F

    b. _____ S F

    c. _____ S F

11. Which state besides Missouri was formed by the Missouri Compromise?

12. Identify two slave states from which a slave could escape directly across the Ohio River into a free state.

13. The shortest route by land for the Underground Railroad from Maryland to Canada would pass through which two free states?

Show You Know

14. Complete each of the sensory figures below. For each figure,

- write statements describing something each figure saw, heard, touched, and felt (emotions) during the time period covered in this chapter.

- include and underline at least one of the historical terms below in each of your statements. Use each term once.

Historical terms: Missouri Compromise, free state, slave state, abolitionists, Underground Railroad, Compromise of 1850, "Bleeding Kansas," Abraham Lincoln, Confederacy

Station A Label

Station A Directions

General Meade's Headquarters (Military Tactics and Technology)

1. Learn about this site. You are standing in front of the headquarters of General George Meade, a commander of one of the Union armies. This is where General Meade directs the actions of the more than 85,000 Union soldiers under his command at Gettysburg. Show respect for General Meade by standing upright and saluting his image on Placard 19A.

2. Read Section 19.4 of your book. Then add illustrations and notes to the drawings of the two soldiers on your Reading Notes. Follow these directions:
   - Next to the Confederate soldier, draw a telegraph pole with wires. Then explain how the South used the telegraph during the Civil War.
   - Next to the Union soldier, draw a simple trench. Then explain why trenches were useful to Union soldiers in battle.

3. Complete the task described below.
   - Look off into the distance. "See" smoke rising from the town of Gettysburg. "See" that the Union army has been driven from the town. "See" that a part of the Confederate army has advanced southward onto Seminary Ridge.
   - Examine the map of the Gettysburg battlefield on July 1. Note the locations of the Confederate forces. Your task is to identify for General Meade the best positions for the Union army to occupy at this point in the fighting.
   - On the map, place the troop markers in the best positions for the Union army to occupy.

4. Check your answer. Lift this page to check your answer. Then return the materials to the condition in which you found them.

Station A Material: Map Answer Key

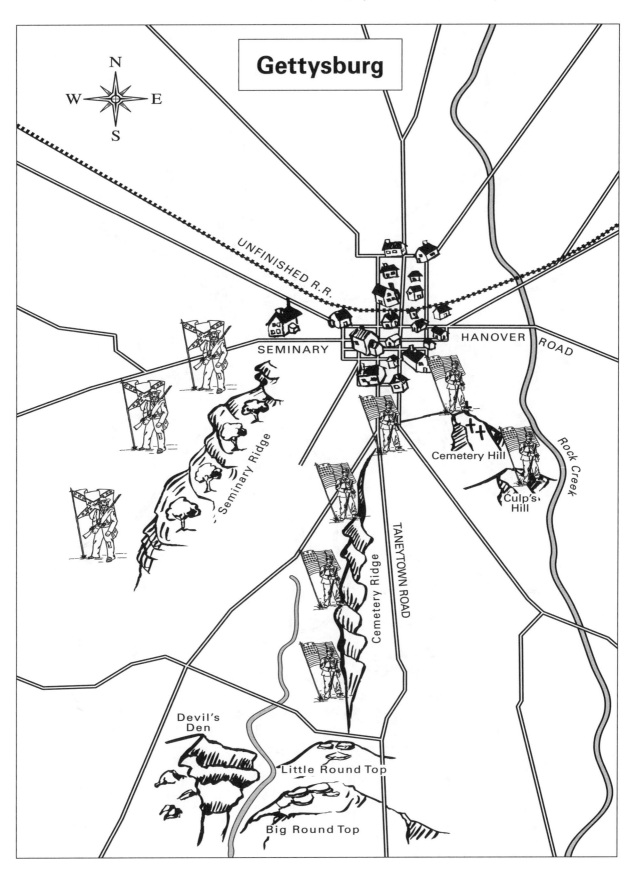

Station A Material: Map of Gettysburg, July 1, 1863

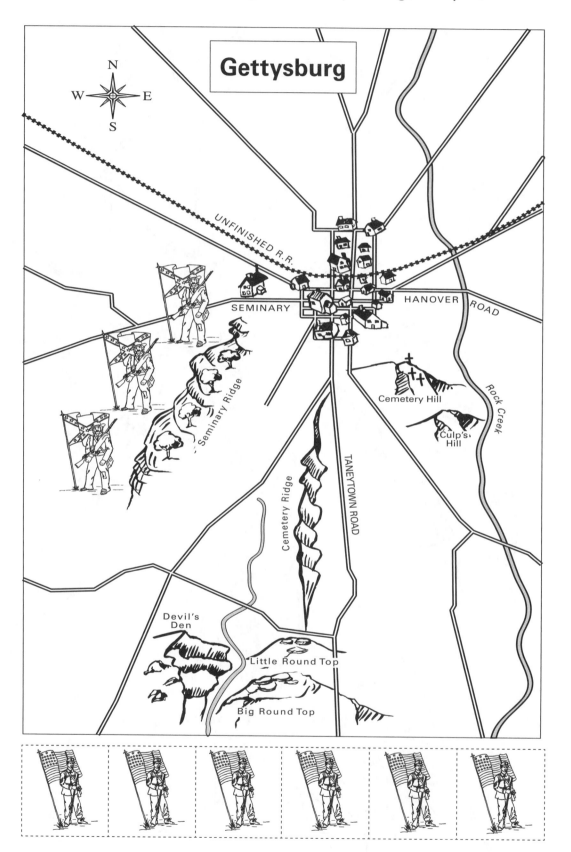

Station B Label

Cemetery Ridge

Station B Directions

Cemetery Ridge (Combat Conditions)

1. Learn about this site. You are dug in with Union troops on Cemetery Ridge. This is a strip of high ground located south of the town of Gettysburg. It is where a daring attack by 15,000 Confederate soldiers is expected to take place. Suppose that these desks are boulders. Crawl over to examine the image of Union soldiers shown on Placard 19B.

2. Read Section 19.5 of your book. Then add illustrations and notes to the drawings of the two soldiers on your Reading Notes. Follow these directions:

- Near the Confederate soldier, draw a simple picture of cannonballs exploding. Then explain what Confederate soldiers often experienced during artillery shelling.
- At the end of the Union soldier's rifle, draw a simple bayonet. Then explain why a Union soldier might have feared a bayonet charge.

3. Complete the task described below.

- Examine the projected image of the Confederate charge on Cemetery Ridge led by General George Pickett.
- Discuss these questions with your partner: *What interesting details do you see in the image? If you were a Union soldier who fought in this battle, how would you describe it to your family? If you were a Confederate soldier, how would you describe it to your family?*
- Read the eyewitness accounts of the Battle of Gettysburg to learn how two soldiers did describe their experiences.
- About 160,000 Union and Confederate soldiers fought at Gettysburg. How many soldiers do you think were killed or wounded during the three days of fighting?

4. Check your answer. Lift this paper to check your answer. Then return the materials to the condition in which you found them.

Answer: 50,000 soldiers

Station B Material: Eyewitness Accounts

Eyewitness Account 1

Man touching man, rank pressing rank . . . the [Confederate] flags wave, their horsemen gallop up and down; the arms of thirteen thousand men, barrel and bayonet, gleam in the sun, a sloping forest of flashing steel.

Right on [the Confederate soldiers] move, as with one soul, in perfect order, over ridge and slope, through orchard and meadow and cornfield, magnificent, grim, irresistible.

Frank Aretas Haskell of the Union army

Eyewitness Account 2

As we ran, a man . . . to my right and rear had his throat cut by a bullet, and he ran past me breathing at his throat and the blood spattering. . . . My dead and wounded were then nearly as great in number as those still on duty. They literally covered the ground. . . . The blood stood in puddles in some places on the rocks; the ground was soaked with blood.

Colonel William C. Oates of the Confederate army

Station C Label

Station C Directions

Surgeon's Tent (Medical Care)

1. Learn about this site. You are standing inside a Union army surgeon's tent at Gettysburg. Here, surgeons and nurses treat wounded soldiers. Walk over and examine the image of the inside of a surgeon's tent, on Placard 19C. As you view the image, act out swatting at flies that have been attracted by the filthy conditions in the tent.

2. Read Section 19.6 of your book. Then add illustrations and notes to the drawings of the two soldiers on your Reading Notes. Follow these directions:

- Around the leg of the Confederate soldier, draw a simple splint made of a tree branch. Then explain what doctors and nurses did when manufactured medical supplies were unavailable.
- Next to the Union soldier, draw a simple medicine bottle. Then describe the problems with the medicines given to troops.

3. Complete the task described below.

- Pretend that one of you is a surgeon and one of you is a soldier wounded in combat.
- Patient, draw a Wound Card from the pile and show it to your surgeon. Then lie on the ground at the station while the surgeon reads the card aloud. Act like you are in great pain.
- Surgeon, examine the medical supplies shown on the sheet. Identify which you would use to treat the wound your patient has.
- Surgeon, take a strip of paper and wrap it around the limb nearest to the patient's wound. Secure the paper with a piece of tape.
- Patient, draw a Fate Card from the pile and follow the directions.

4. Check your answer. Lift the flap and check that you chose the correct instrument to treat the wound. Then shuffle the cards and return the materials to the condition in which you found them.

Answers:
Wound Card 1: bone saw
Wound Card 2: bullet probe
Wound Card 3: tourniquet
Wound Card 4: splint

Station C Material: Medical Instruments

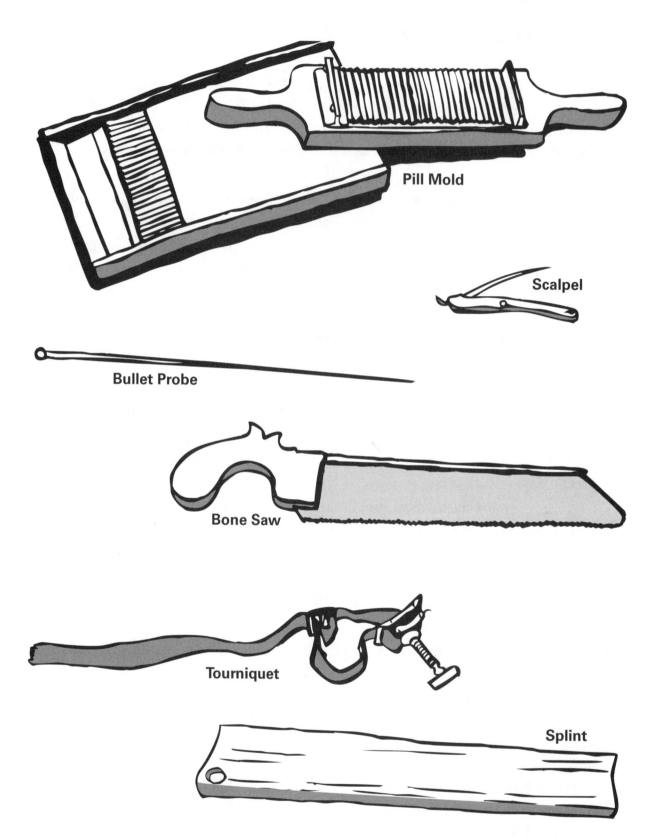

Pill Mold

Scalpel

Bullet Probe

Bone Saw

Tourniquet

Splint

Station C Material: Wound Cards

Wound Card 1

Your **foot** has become infected after an operation. The surgeon must act quickly to prevent the infection from spreading throughout your body.

Wound Card 2

You were shot in the **leg** during battle. The bullet is causing you great pain. You want the surgeon to remove it as quickly as possible.

Wound Card 3

You were hit in the **arm** with a piece of shrapnel (a small piece of metal) from a cannonball. An artery (a major blood vessel) in your arm is bleeding. The surgeon must stop the bleeding quickly, or you will die.

Wound Card 4

Your **arm** was broken in a hand-to-hand fight with a Confederate soldier. The surgeon must bind the arm so that it won't move and the bone can heal properly.

Station C Material: Fate Cards

Fate Card	**Fate Card**	**Fate Card**
Like nearly 600,000 Union and Confederate soldiers who fought in the Civil War, you will die from your wounds or from disease. Have your surgeon draw a simple picture of a tombstone on the strip of paper used for your bandage.	Like nearly 600,000 Union and Confederate soldiers who fought in the Civil War, you will die from your wounds or from disease. Have your surgeon draw a simple picture of a tombstone on the strip of paper used for your bandage.	Like nearly 600,000 Union and Confederate soldiers who fought in the Civil War, you will die from your wounds or from disease. Have your surgeon draw a simple picture of a tombstone on the strip of paper used for your bandage.
Fate Card	**Fate Card**	**Fate Card**
You are one of the lucky ones! You will survive your stay in a Civil War hospital. Approximately 24 percent of all soldiers who served in the Civil War died from their wounds or from disease. Shake your surgeon's hand and thank him or her for saving your life.	You are one of the lucky ones! You will survive your stay in a Civil War hospital. Approximately 24 percent of all soldiers who served in the Civil War died from their wounds or from disease. Shake your surgeon's hand and thank him or her for saving your life.	You are one of the lucky ones! You will survive your stay in a Civil War hospital. Approximately 24 percent of all soldiers who served in the Civil War died from their wounds or from disease. Shake your surgeon's hand and thank him or her for saving your life.

Fate Card

Like nearly 600,000 Union and Confederate soldiers who fought in the Civil War, you will die from your wounds or from disease. Have your surgeon draw a simple picture of a tombstone on the strip of paper used for your bandage.

Fate Card

Like nearly 600,000 Union and Confederate soldiers who fought in the Civil War, you will die from your wounds or from disease. Have your surgeon draw a simple picture of a tombstone on the strip of paper used for your bandage.

Fate Card

Like nearly 600,000 Union and Confederate soldiers who fought in the Civil War, you will die from your wounds or from disease. Have your surgeon draw a simple picture of a tombstone on the strip of paper used for your bandage.

Fate Card

You are one of the lucky ones! You will survive your stay in a Civil War hospital. Approximately 24 percent of all soldiers who served in the Civil War died from their wounds or from disease. Shake your surgeon's hand and thank him or her for saving your life.

Fate Card

You are one of the lucky ones! You will survive your stay in a Civil War hospital. Approximately 24 percent of all soldiers who served in the Civil War died from their wounds or from disease. Shake your surgeon's hand and thank him or her for saving your life.

Fate Card

You are one of the lucky ones! You will survive your stay in a Civil War hospital. Approximately 24 percent of all soldiers who served in the Civil War died from their wounds or from disease. Shake your surgeon's hand and thank him or her for saving your life.

Station D Label

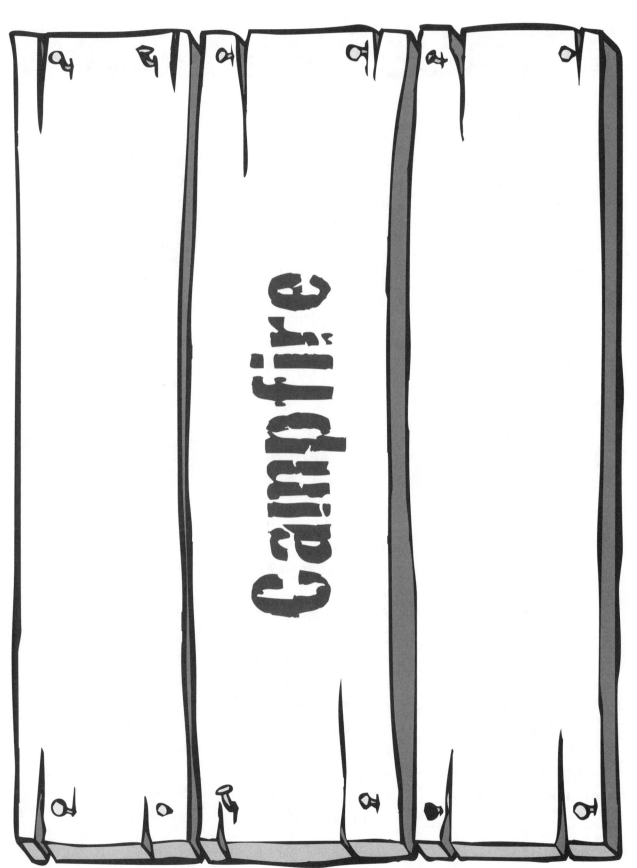

Station D Directions

Campfire (Food and Drink)

1. Learn about this site. You are standing near a Union army campfire at Gettysburg. Some of the soldiers gather here to eat their meals. Walk over to the image on Placard 19D of soldiers waiting for food. As you examine the image, hold your stomach occasionally, as though you have a stomachache.

2. Read Section 19.7 of your book. Then add illustrations and notes to the drawings of the two soldiers on your Reading Notes. Follow these directions:

- In one hand of the Confederate soldier, draw an apple. Then explain why Confederate soldiers, like other soldiers, often had to steal food.
- In one hand of the Union soldier, draw a hardtack biscuit. Then describe some of the other food supplies that Union soldiers commonly received during the Civil War.

3. Complete the task described below.

- Take one of the "hardtack biscuits."
- Sit down on the ground next to the campfire, and "eat" the hardtack. Picture other soldiers sitting near you.
- Play CD Track 9, "Hard Tack Come Again No More." Take a copy of the lyrics and sing along with the song as it is playing.
- After listening to the recording, answer this question: *Why did the words of the song change to "O, hard tack, come again once more"?*

4. Check your answer. Lift the flap to check your answer. Then return the materials to the condition in which you found them.

Answer: The horse feed the cooks call mush is even worse than hardtack.

Station D Material: Hardtack Biscuits

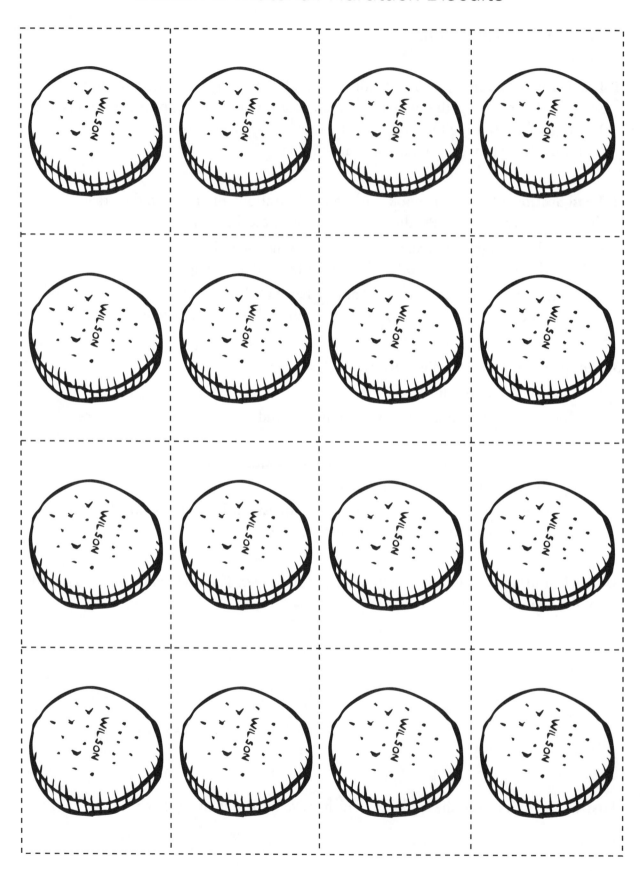

Station D Material: "Hard Tack Come Again No More"

Hard Tack Come Again No More

Let us close our game of poker, take our tin cups in our hand
  As we all stand by the cook's tent door
As dried monies of hard crackers are handed to each man.
  O, hard tack, come again no more!

Chorus: 'Tis the song, the sigh of the hungry:
  "O, hard tack, hard tack, come again no more."
Many days you have lingered upon our stomachs sore.
  O, hard tack, come again no more!

'Tis the wail that is heard in camp both night and day,
  'Tis the murmur that's mingled with each snore.
'Tis the sighing of the soul for spring chickens far away,
  O, hard tack, come again no more!

Chorus: 'Tis the song, the sigh of the hungry:
  "O, hard tack, hard tack, come again no more."
Many days you have lingered upon our stomachs sore.
  O, hard tack, come again no more!

But to all these cries and murmurs, there comes a sudden hush
  As frail forms are fainting by the door,
For they feed us now on horse feed that the cooks call mush!
  O, hard tack, come again once more!

Final Chorus: 'Tis the song, the sigh of the starving:
  "O, hard tack, hard tack, come again once more!"
You were old and very wormy, but we pass your failings o'er.
  O, hard tack, come again once more!

Station E Label

Station E Directions

Postal Wagon (Conditions on the Home Front)

1. Learn about this site. You are standing next to a postal wagon stopped on Taneytown Road, which leads into Gettysburg. Soldiers often come to wagons like these to pick up letters from friends and family members back home. Walk over and examine the image of the postal wagon on Placard 19E. As you do, show that you are homesick by dabbing tears that have welled up in your eyes.

2. Read Section 19.8 of your book. Then add illustrations and notes to the drawings of the two soldiers on your Reading Notes. Follow these directions:

- Above the head of the Confederate soldier, draw a thought bubble. In the thought bubble, describe the soldier's feelings about the effects of food shortages in the South during the Civil War.
- Above the head of the Union soldier, draw a thought bubble. In the thought bubble, describe the soldier's feelings about the draft riots that took place in the North during the Civil War.

3. Complete the task described below.

- Take one letter from the "mailbag."
- Turn away from your partner. Sit on the ground or lean against a wall (as if it is a tree) so that you can read your letter privately.
- Read the letter. Try to determine whether it describes conditions in the North or the South during the Civil War.

4. Check your answer. Lift the flap to check your answer. Then return the materials to the condition in which you found them.

Answers: Letters 1 and 2 describe conditions in the North. Letters 3 and 4 describe conditions in the South.

Station E Material: Letters from the Home Front

Letter 1

Dear Louis,

How is it with you? The children are fine, but they miss you badly—as do I. I know you are worried about our printing business. However, things are running smoothly under my leadership.

But enough about us. I must inform you of a serious event that recently took place in our city. It seems that many here are opposed to the new draft law. In protest, thousands of men and women took to the streets the other day. There was screaming and swearing in the most frantic manner. Eventually, the crowd set the Colored Orphan Asylum on fire. When firemen arrived to try to extinguish the blaze, their hoses were cut, and the firemen were badly beaten. How do your comrades feel about the draft law?

Your faithful wife,
Ellen

Letter 2

Dear Seymour,

I hope that all is well with you. My work at the ammunition factory leaves me exhausted at the end of the day. Then there are the children to tend to. Still, I want to pass along some exciting news.

The president has authorized the use of black troops in our army. If anyone had predicted that last year, they would have been called a fool. Plans are being made in our state to organize a regiment of black soldiers. Some people are opposed to this plan because they think blacks cannot be trained to be soldiers. I disagree. What group better recognizes that this war is about ending slavery? Don't you agree?

Your devoted wife,
Amy

Letter 3

Dear Robert,

I got your affectionate letter yesterday. It gives me great relief of mind to hear that you are alive and well.

I also got a letter from my sister, Elizabeth. Although our husbands are fighting against each other in this awful war, she tries to stay in touch. It sounds as if she faces far more difficult hardships than those I suffer. She says that food there is in short supply. Every day, her government gives out only one half of a peck of corn to each soldier's wife. Once, she had to steal extra corn to feed herself and her children. It is hard to think of my sister—that honorable woman—having to resort to such measures. I hate to think about how hard it must be to obtain other things, such as medicine and clothing. How can they keep fighting with such tenacity?

Your devoted wife,
Mary

Letter 4

Dear Alexander,

I know that you and your brother have not spoken since the start of this war. It is sad that politics have caused you to fight in two different armies. But I thought that you might want to know about what conditions are like in his town.

Your brother told us that some soldiers fighting for your cause looted his house the other day. They took all of the chickens and the turkeys they could find. At one point, they even rolled out the family carriage and filled it with chickens. Later, his wife caught some troops—against their officer's orders—stuffing their pockets with pieces of silverware. Although the soldiers took all the things of value that they could find, your brother was thankful that they didn't burn his house to the ground. Had his home been in the path of General Sherman's army, things might have turned out far worse. Why must your army destroy so much property during this war?

Your humble father,
Thomas

Writing a Eulogy for Gettysburg Soldiers

A eulogy is a speech or written piece that praises a person or thing. Write a eulogy honoring all those who fought and died at Gettysburg. Your eulogy should include

- a description of the conditions under which Union and Confederate soldiers fought and died.
- the following terms: *freedom, Pickett's Charge, trenches, artillery shells, wounded, hardtack, shortages, Appomattox.*
- a serious, dramatic tone.
- no spelling or grammatical errors.

Chapter 19 Assessment

Big Ideas
Fill in the circle next to the best answer.

1. The Emancipation Proclamation was an order to
   - ○ A. free slaves in the South.
   - ○ B. leave the Union.
   - ○ C. protect the homeland.
   - ○ D. keep the country together.

2. What was the purpose of the draft?
   - ○ A. to destroy railroads
   - ○ B. to improve training
   - ○ C. to provide better food
   - ○ D. to get enough soldiers

3. The phrase "the blue and the gray" refers to
   - ○ A. battleships.
   - ○ B. hospitals.
   - ○ C. technology.
   - ○ D. uniforms.

4. Unlike most Civil War battles, the Battle of Gettysburg
   - ○ A. ended the Civil War.
   - ○ B. took place in the North.
   - ○ C. resulted in very few deaths.
   - ○ D. was won by the Confederacy.

5. Which tactics and technology did not help defenders in battles?
   - ○ A. positions on low ground
   - ○ B. hot-air balloons
   - ○ C. trenches and dirt walls
   - ○ D. rifles and artillery

6. What was the greatest cause of death for Civil War soldiers?
   - ○ A. bayonets ○ C. gunshots
   - ○ B. disease ○ D. poison

7. Why did workers riot in New York City in 1863?
   - ○ A. They were running out of food.
   - ○ B. They wanted to stop making weapons.
   - ○ C. They did not want to be forced to fight.
   - ○ D. They believed the slaves should be freed.

8. What happened at Appomattox?
   - ○ A. Pickett's Charge failed.
   - ○ B. Lincoln freed the slaves.
   - ○ C. Lee surrendered to Grant.
   - ○ D. Ships with iron sides fought.

Reading Further
9. What was the process by which Congress tried to rebuild the South and reunite it with the Union?
   - ○ A. Abolition
   - ○ B. Assassination
   - ○ C. Ratification
   - ○ D. Reconstruction

10. Sharecroppers rented farmland by giving the landowner
    - ○ A. 40 acres and a mule.
    - ○ B. part of what they grew.
    - ○ C. wages they earned in town.
    - ○ D. payments toward buying the land.

Social Studies Skills

Read this part of a Confederate soldier's letter home. The soldier wrote the letter in northern Georgia in July 1864. Use the letter to answer the questions below.

> Dear Sister,
> Pickets [guard soldiers] don't fire at each other now. We go down to the edge of the river on our side and the Yankees come down on their side and talk to each other. The men on picket opposite are from Ohio, and seem very tired of the war. . . . Gen. Johnson has issued an order that there shall be no more communication with them . . . The Yankees are very much in want of tobacco, and our Government gives it to us, and we used to trade tobacco with them for knives and canteens [water bottles]. There is a rock near the middle of the river to which they would swim and trade. . . . That has been broken up now and if any trading is carried on, it is done contrary to orders.

11. According to the letter, how did the Union soldiers feel about the war?

12. Write a word or phrase that describes how the soldiers on both sides felt toward each other, as shown in the letter.

13. For what reason do you think General Johnson might have issued the order mentioned in the letter?

14. According to this letter, why did soldiers in opposing armies trade with each other?

Show You Know

15. During their spare time, Civil War soldiers often rewrote the lyrics (words) to well-known songs of the period to describe some aspect of their experience. The song "Hard Tack Come Again No More"—originally titled "Hard Times Come No More"—is an example. Suppose that you are a Civil War soldier writing lyrics to a familiar song to describe your experience. Follow these steps:

- Think of a well-known song with a simple tune that most of the other "soldiers" in your class know (such as "Row, Row, Row Your Boat" or "Old MacDonald").

- On a separate sheet of paper, write new lyrics to the song. The lyrics should describe one aspect of the soldier's experience you studied in this chapter—military tactics and technology, combat conditions, medical care, food and drink, or conditions on the home front.

- Your lyrics should be at least six lines and include at least three interesting or important facts about the aspect of the soldier's experience you chose to describe.

- Create a new, appropriate title for your song. Underneath the title, write: *Sung to the tune of "[name of the well-known song you chose]."*

Example: "A Confederate Soldier's Daily Rations"
Sung to the tune of "Row, Row, Row Your Boat"

Pick-, pick-, pickled meat
Hardtack, chic-o-ry
This is what I get to eat
If I am luck-, luck-y.

Timeline Pictures

Timeline Summaries

- The United States and the _____ distrusted each other.
- The two superpowers struggled over the best type of government and way of life.
- Many people died in wars between communists and noncommunists.
- Supplies of _____ increased.

- _____ became the most popular form of entertainment.
- Computers did people's work accurately and quickly.
- The _____ and the World Wide Web made it easy to obtain information.

- Germany, led by _____, and Japan attacked their neighbors.
- Hitler and his followers hated certain peoples, including _____.
- The United States dropped atomic bombs on _____.

- The nation struggled to give all citizens equal rights.
- A movement was started to end _____ in the South.
- _____ encouraged nonviolent protests.
- Other groups began to fight against _____ _____.

- The stock market _____.
- Banks closed.
- A drought ruined crops. Many farmers lost their _____.
- People lost their jobs.

- Machines made goods that people had once made for themselves.
- People moved from farms to _____ for jobs.
- Improvements in _____ made travel easier.

- Competition and mistrust caused the war.
- Soldiers fought from ditches called _____.
- The treaty that ended the war made _____ give up land and pay damages.

Card Game Illustrations

Card Game Information

Machines made goods that people had once made for themselves.	People lost their jobs.	The nation struggled to give all citizens equal rights.
People moved from farms to cities for jobs.	Hitler and his followers hated certain peoples, including Jews.	Martin Luther King Jr. encouraged nonviolent protests.
Soldiers fought from ditches called trenches.	The United States dropped atomic bombs on Japan.	Television became the most popular form of entertainment.
The treaty that ended the war made Germany give up land and pay damages.	Supplies of nuclear weapons increased.	The Internet and the World Wide Web made it easy to obtain information.
The stock market crashed.	The two superpowers struggled over the best type of government and way of life.	

Chapter 20 Assessment

Big Ideas

Fill in the circle next to the best answer.

1. As a result of industrialization, many people moved
   - ○ A. from farms to cities.
   - ○ B. from the United States to Europe.
   - ○ C. from suburbs to small towns.
   - ○ D. from the West Coast to the East.

2. Why did people begin to buy clothes in stores?
   - ○ A. Schools did not teach sewing.
   - ○ B. Factories made clothes cheaply.
   - ○ C. Homemade clothes looked bad.
   - ○ D. Some towns did not have a tailor.

3. World War I began as a conflict between nations in
   - ○ A. Africa.
   - ○ B. Asia.
   - ○ C. Europe.
   - ○ D. South America.

4. Large numbers of workers lost their jobs and their homes because of the
   - ○ A. Cold War.
   - ○ B. Great Depression.
   - ○ C. World War II.
   - ○ D. civil rights movement.

5. Which country attacked American ships at Pearl Harbor, Hawaii, in 1941?
   - ○ A. China
   - ○ B. Germany
   - ○ C. Italy
   - ○ D. Japan

6. The Cold War was called "cold" because the United States and the Soviet Union
   - ○ A. flew over the North Pole.
   - ○ B. were enemies for a long time.
   - ○ C. stopped speaking to each other.
   - ○ D. did not fight each other directly.

7. Under segregation in the South, laws and customs before the 1950s
   - ○ A. took land away from farmers.
   - ○ B. created many good factory jobs.
   - ○ C. separated black people and white people.
   - ○ D. required men to serve in the army.

8. Which invention was first developed during the Information Age?
   - ○ A. computers
   - ○ B. electric lights
   - ○ C. railroads
   - ○ D. skyscrapers

Reading Further

9. Trong and Thanh left their home at the end of
   - ○ A. World War I.
   - ○ B. World War II.
   - ○ C. the Vietnam War.
   - ○ D. the Cold War.

10. What is the most important reason refugees move to the United States?
    - ○ A. to be safe
    - ○ B. to get a job
    - ○ C. to go to school
    - ○ D. to learn English

Social Studies Skills

Look at the picture of Brooklyn Bridge in New York City about 1883.
Use the picture to answer the questions.

11. How is the means of transportation in the picture different from most means of transportation in cities today?

12. What is one way in which the picture shows the effects of the industrialization?

13. Why do you think the bridge in the picture might have been difficult to build?

Show You Know

14. Review the key changes and time periods of the 20th and 21st centuries that you studied in this chapter. Think about the ways in which these have had an effect on your life today. On a separate piece of paper, create a cartoon strip of four boxes. Your cartoon should

- have an appropriate title.

- show four ways in which your life has been affected by four of the key changes or time periods of the 20th and 21st centuries described in this chapter. Each box of the comic strip should represent an effect on your life by a different time period.

- include voice and thought bubbles.

Photographs

Cover: RF/Getty Images
Title page: RF/Getty Images
11: National Museum of The American Indian /Smithsonian Institution **44:** The Granger Collection,New York **109:** Yale University Art Gallery **112:** Library of Congress **204:** *Brooklyn Bridge,* circa 1883. Photoengraving by Shugg Brothers

Art

34: Gary Undercuffler **35:** Gary Undercuffler **36:** Gary Undercuffler **86:** Carol Heyer **88:** Carol Heyer **118:** Gary Undercuffler **119:** Gary Undercuffler **120:** Gary Undercuffler **121:** Gary Undercuffler **122:** Gary Undercuffler **129:** Gary Undercuffler **146:** Doug Roy **171:** Susan Jaekel **199:** Susan Jaekel **201:** Susan Jaekel

Artists represented by Ann Remen-Willis, Artist Representative and Art Manager:
Carol Heyer
Susan Jaekel
Doug Roy
Gary Undercuffler